103
Additional Training Games

103
Additional
Training Games

Gary Kroehnert

The McGraw-Hill Companies, Inc.

Sydney New York San Francisco Auckland
Bangkok Bogotá Caracas Hong Kong
Kuala Lumpur Lisbon London Madrid
Mexico City Milan New Delhi San Juan
Seoul Singapore Taipei Toronto

McGraw·Hill Australia

A Division of The McGraw·Hill Companies

National Library of Australia Cataloguing-in-Publication data:

Kroehnert, Gary.
103 additional training games.

ISBN 0 074 71050 8.

1. Management games – Study and teaching. 2. Employees –
Training of. I. Title.

658.312404

Published in Australia by
McGraw-Hill Australia Pty Ltd
4 Barcoo Street, Roseville NSW 2069, Australia
Acquisitions Editor: Javier Dopico
Production Editor: Megan Lowe
Editor: Megan Lowe
Designer (cover and interior): R.T.J. Klinkhamer
Illustrator: Di Booth
Typeset in 10/14 Bell Gothic by R.T.J. Klinkhamer
Printed on 80 gsm woodfree by Prowell Productions Ltd, Hong Kong.

Contents

THE GAMES

CONTENTS

CONTENTS

Introduction

Welcome to my fourth book of training games. **100 Training Games**, **101 More Training Games** and **102 Extra Training Games** were so popular that a fourth book had to be added to the collection. So here it is, **103 Additional Training Games**. That brings us to a grand total of 406 games!

Each game in this book falls into at least one of the following ten categories: Icebreakers, Team building, Communication, Perception, Facilitator/presentation skills, Mid-course energiser, Problem solving, Learning, Evaluation and Self-management. These categories cover all aspects of training.

As the introduction in **100 Training Games**, **101 More Training Games** and **102 Extra Training Games** is still current and relevant, I am using it here again. So if you've already read it, skip it, and go straight to the games section.

We have all seen and probably participated in various forms of training games, simulations, role-plays, brain teasers, case studies and other related activities. Just because we are aware of them doesn't mean that we can use them any time we wish to.

The use of these activities should allow the participant to discover outcomes, rather than be told everything without trying it. Most of the world's airlines, manufacturing plants, human resource companies, military establishments, small and large companies, private and public organisations now use these forms of structured exercises. The ultimate goal of using these structured exercises should always be improved learning.

Trainers and participants are changing. People attending training courses generally don't want to get involved with exercises that are too 'touchy feely'. Most of the trainers that I know personally don't like using exercises where participants have to stare each other in the eye or start hugging each other. For that reason all of the exercises included in this book are 'hands on' and 'down to earth'.

What these trainers and participants are generally interested in, on top of the information sessions, are structured experiences that they can apply, where no one feels very threatened or where they don't have to touch strangers. The other very important criterion that almost everyone agrees on is that the experience should be relevant to the training matter or relevant to the group's requirements.

All facilitators using structured exercises need to be aware that other things may come out in the use of games that normally wouldn't come out using other methods of instruction.

Games, simulations, role-plays, brain teasers, case studies and other related activities have been used successfully in countless numbers of training situations for many centuries by countless numbers of trainers. We can actually trace back the use of games and simulations thousands of years. Chess is an excellent example of this. Chess was developed by the military and was based on solving military problems.

Games, simulations, role-plays, brain teasers, case studies and other related activities have also been used unsuccessfully in countless numbers of training situations for many centuries by countless numbers of trainers.

For most of us, games, simulations and role-plays were part of the growing up process. If we think back to our earliest school days, we can remember playing games such as marbles or hide-and-seek. It is now recognised that these games are not only for fun, but also prepare the child for entry into the social system. If any of you took Home Economics, Woodwork or Metalwork at school you would probably call them a simulation of the real workplace. Some of us may also remember when we acted out roles in a game of 'Mothers and Fathers'—another form of role-play.

In a training situation we must be very selective in the use and timing of these methods of instruction. People become bored doing the same thing all the time, even if it is a 'mind-blowing experience' the first few times. If you intend using these methods effectively, plan them into your session notes or your outline.

This book, and my previous games books, are aimed at giving both the new and the experienced trainer enough information, samples and sources to competently carry out their role as an adult trainer using these related training activities. They all focus primarily on games and brain teasers, as role-plays and case studies have to be designed by the individual trainer for each separate application. For the new trainer I would strongly suggest that they also spend some time looking at my training handbook, **Basic Training for Trainers**, Third Edition (McGraw-Hill Australia, Sydney, 2000).

Today's trainer can simply walk down to the local shopping centre and purchase any number of games over the counter. It's worth mentioning now that even the simplest child's game can have a place in adult education if it's applied correctly.

Training games are now found in all sections of all kinds of education. It's important that the trainer realises, however, that a game is not played just because someone else has said, 'There should be a game played here.'

In **103 Additional Training Games** we will first look at the academic differences between games, simulations, brain teasers, role-plays and case studies. We will also address the problem of when to use training games. The largest (and most important) section of the book is a selection of favourite training games and brain teasers. Near the end of the book you will find a series of 'Observer's Sheets'. These can be used to help observers focus on what it is they are supposed to be looking for. Last, an updated bibliography is included for new trainers to use as a resource and for their further reference.

It's worthwhile noting that trainers and facilitators these days tend to call all these activities 'structured experiences' or 'structured exercises'. So when you hear these terms being used you will know that they are still talking about the same things. I have mostly referred to games, simulations, brain teasers and role-plays as exercises or activities. To me the term is not that important as long as the trainer knows what the desired outcome is.

Most of the exercises are written as directions, rather than in the third person; however, where necessary I refer to the leader as the facilitator rather than as the trainer. In most structured exercises it's important for the leader not to be a dominant figure. Generally, if you use the term 'facilitator', that lets the group know that they aren't going to be taught by a trainer but rather find out for themselves through experience.

With the exercises contained in this handbook I would suggest that the reader/user apply common sense to use the enlarging facilities on their photocopier to make appropriate sized overhead transparencies. This will save presentation time by reducing the writing required on the whiteboard, etc. All of the overhead material has been shown in landscape format (i.e. wider than it is deep) as this has become the most common way of projecting overheads. It's also the easiest way for people to read them.

My policy for reproducing any material from this handbook is based on encouraging interprofessional networking. Therefore the material contained in this book may be freely reproduced for educational purposes or training activities. You are not required to obtain special permission for such uses. It is requested, however, that the following statement appear on all copies made:

Reproduced from:
103 Additional Training Games, Gary Kroehnert,
McGraw-Hill Australia, Sydney,
Copyright 2001

Finally I would like to thank all the authors, game designers and publishers who have allowed me to use their material for the benefit of new trainers.

I have attempted to acknowledge the source wherever possible. Where a source hasn't been acknowledged, either the source is unknown to me or my colleagues, or it's an original game design. As it's next to impossible to find the source of a story or a game on most occasions, I will now apologise if I have not acknowledged the source, or if it has been acknowledged incorrectly.

If you have any games or exercises that you would like to share with other trainers, please send them to me for possible inclusion in future publications (**104 New Training Games** is currently being thought about). Your name will be immortalised, as I will acknowledge the source. If possible, please try to use the same format as shown here. For those who are interested my contact details are shown below.

Before we start looking at the games, just remember what Confucius said around 450BC:

'I hear and I forget,
I see and I remember,
I do and I understand.'

Have fun!

Dr Gary Kroehnert 2001
PO Box 3169
Grose Vale
New South Wales 2753
Australia
Phone: (02) 4572 2000
Fax: (02) 4572 2200
Email: doctorgary@hotmail.com

The Activities

THE DIFFERENCES BETWEEN THEM

Very few trainers agree on definitions for games, simulations and role-plays, case studies, and so on. The following definitions are very broad and have been included for a new trainer to use. The more experience a trainer gains, the more they can apply their own definitions.

By looking at some of the examples given here, you will be able to see that it's difficult to even categorise some exercises into one grouping. Chess, for example, isn't strictly a game or a simulation, it's a combination of both. Chess was developed in sixth century India and was designed to simulate a contemporary battle.

Games

A game is an exercise where participants are involved in a contest with someone else (or a group of people) with a set of rules imposed. Games normally include some type of pay-off. Most training games are now aimed at having the individual trainee compete with themselves, rather than with another trainee. This avoids the situation where there are winners and losers.

The term 'games' includes psychomotor skills games, intellectual skills games and most games of chance. Some common types of games include darts, snakes and ladders, football, Scrabble, charades and most card games. Games in which individuals compete with themselves include solitaire, patience, crossword puzzles and even poker machines.

Simulations

A simulation is a mock-up of an actual or imaginary situation. Simulations are generally used to train future operators where it's impractical or too dangerous for these trainees to use real-life equipment or locations. Simulations are normally designed to be as realistic as possible so that trainees can learn from their actions without the financial worries of repairing or replacing damaged equipment.

Examples of simulations include flight simulators, driving simulators and war games.

Brain Teasers

Brain teasers are in a class of their own. They are neither pure games nor simulations but puzzles that either keep participants' minds busy or highlight key points. Brain teasers generally don't have any rules, but they do allow the trainer to design their own rules to suit the individual training session.

Typical brain teasers include exercises such as joining the dots and most perception exercises.

Role-plays

Role-plays are used in training to see how participants react in certain situations before and after training sessions. Role-plays are very useful in getting participants used to dealing with other people in any given scenario. Even when the participant does it wrong, they still learn.

Case Studies

Case studies are exactly what the name implies. A case (normally from the participants' workplace) is studied either by the group or by the individual. An in-depth study of a real-life or simulated scenario is undertaken to illustrate certain outcomes. When the group or the individual has the answer to the problem or situation it can be compared to what really happened and what the outcomes were.

WHEN SHOULD THEY BE USED?

Training exercises may be used at any time during the training as long as they are relevant, to the point or have been designed with a specific purpose.

The 'specific purpose' can be to keep the group occupied while waiting for stragglers, and to wake participants up after a lunch break. These purposes are okay as long as they are stated. It's not okay when they are simply used to fill in time or to make the facilitator look like a magician.

You can also use structured exercises as a means of channelling excess energy or to liven up the class. The activity can be a means of improving the learning atmosphere.

So these types of structured exercises should be selected and used on the basis of their usefulness, for reinforcing the instruction, or improving the learning environment.

A FACILITATOR'S RESPONSIBILITIES?

Gone are the days when games and the like were not considered to be suitable as training methods. Training is a serious business, but we can and should use games, simulations, role-plays, brain teasers, case studies and other related activities in training situations.

War games (simulations) have been used by military personnel for many centuries and have proved to be very effective. Structured exercises are relatively new to training, and they are also proving to be very effective, if used properly.

Regardless of how good we are as presenters or lecturers, we can't fool ourselves into thinking that our whole presentation alone is going to keep everyone's interest for the whole period. Games, simulations, role-plays, brain teasers, case studies and other related activities are all applications of the principles of adult learning. You, the facilitator, must ensure that the participants do not become so involved in the activity that they actually miss the learning point. In addition, the facilitator must also realise that if the participants have too high a level of enthusiasm for the exercise they may become bored with 'normal' training. This isn't to say that we don't want high levels of enthusiasm, but we need to ensure we keep the participants interested with other methods of instruction as well.

The learning process can be sped up by the use of games, simulations, role-plays, brain teasers, case studies and other related activities. People learn better when they are enjoying themselves. So therefore we need to seriously think about creating or supplying the appropriate learning atmosphere.

You should always select the training method after setting the learning objectives. The method should respond to the participants' needs, not the facilitator's.

When you decide to use a structured exercise it is important that you practise the exercise at least once with a group of people not involved with the immediate presentation. This will help you see if the design is going to work, and in the expected way with the expected results. Like all types of training, these structured exercises must be evaluated for their worth and effectiveness. If they don't produce what is needed, you need to scrap them or modify them.

Do you have a responsibility for entertaining the group during any presentation? You have the responsibility for ensuring clarity and precision of information. You are also responsible for aligning the group and keep them moving. Another responsibility is to keep yourself animated. (That could be considered the main entertainment value.) This is also what the participants may talk about later to their friends and colleagues. If the facilitator is in a situation where this type of feedback is required (such as an external trainer or consultant), then an assortment of training methods will be required. Games, simulations, role-plays and structured exercises will be of assistance.

It's your responsibility to pilot or test all new exercises or exercises that you haven't used in the past. Facilitators must realise that what works for some people doesn't always work for others. A lot of training exercises may have different outcomes every time you use them. So be prepared.

Trainers and facilitators must debrief all the exercises carried out during any type of training session. The purpose of debriefing is quite complicated. Without going into too much detail, there are two main reasons for conducting the debriefing session.

You have an obligation to put the players or participants back together when the exercise has finished. This means that if participants have bad feelings about the exercise they should be allowed to get things off their chest while still in the training room and also while things are still fresh in their minds.

Debriefing also allows the trainer and the participants to talk about the outcomes of the exercise. Was it what everyone expected? Would you do that in the real situation? What would you have done if this had happened? It also allows the trainer a time where mistakes can be corrected.

Put the participants back together if you shatter them, or scrape them off the floor.

Probably the most important point is that trainers must be completely honest and open with their participants. This includes not having any hidden agendas, not misleading participants, not setting anyone up, not deceiving any of the participants and not using the participants' efforts for your own gain.

WHERE CAN THEY BE USED?

Rather than fully catalogue these exercises and possibly limit their application, I have decided to use a coding system. Beside the name of the exercises on the following pages you will see one or some of the following letters and symbols. These letters have been placed there to give you suggested applications. **These applications are only guides and can be modified to suit by the individual trainer.**

Coding:

I   Icebreaker
T   Team building
C   Communication
F   Facilitator/presentation skills
M   Mid-course energiser
X   Problem solving
L   Learning
P   Perception
E   Evaluation
S   Self-management

A full breakdown of the exercises has been included on the next few pages of this handbook. First, each of the ten different categories has been given a detailed overview. The second list is an index of the 103 exercises included in this book, with full cross-referencing for each application for which they can be used.

I Icebreaker

Almost any exercise can be used as an icebreaker. The two main purposes of using an icebreaker are first, to allow the participants to introduce themselves to each other, and second, to lead into the topic matter. Participants often find that the topic matter is made clearer by the use of an appropriate icebreaker.

The exercises in this grouping are non-threatening introductory contacts. They are designed to allow participants to get to know each other a little and to lower any barriers that may exist. Experienced facilitators have found that the success or failure of a program may hinge on these two points.

The more comfortable participants feel with each other, the better the learning environment. If the participants are at ease with each other, they are more likely to participate and to generate new ideas.

While most facilitators won't see these exercises as too threatening, some participants may. If a participant does see an icebreaker as threatening, make sure they have a way out of participating. It's a wise decision to let people know at the very beginning of a program that they can pass on any exercise or activity they feel uncomfortable with. Obviously there will be exceptions to this. A trainee counsellor, for example, would not be expected to say that they feel uncomfortable talking with strangers and would prefer not to do any counselling role-plays. Common sense rules.

T Team building

Team-building exercises are used to improve the relationship of the individuals and sub-groups within a group. The term 'group' in team building normally refers to an established work group or a group which will be working together.

When using team-building exercises you, as well as the group, should be aware that the identification of conflict or problems between different parties or individuals may be the only outcome of some team-building exercises. However, a conflict or problem is much easier to solve or deal with after it has been identified. A team-building exercise should allow the participants to 'let their hair down' while they get to know each other.

It's very important that you thoroughly debrief team-building exercises to ensure that there isn't any build up of hostility, anger or frustration. Don't let the group break until this has been rectified.

C Communication

Exercises used for communication are designed to let the participants find out where certain communication skills may be improved. You, as the facilitator, have to be very aware of the exact purpose of some communication exercises as it is sometimes very difficult to sit back and say nothing while things start to go wrong for the participant.

You also need to be aware that you may be regarded by some participants as a role-model. While conducting a program on communication skills you must ensure that what you give out is correct. As feedback is a very important part of communication skills it must be used in all communication exercises. Feedback should be specific and aimed at observed behaviours that the individual has some control over.

F Facilitator/presentation skills

Facilitation skills activities are aimed at people who may need to develop or improve their up-front, or presentation, ability. The exercises in this category are designed to encourage the participants to think about particular aspects of their own presentation and facilitation skills.

While using any exercises to improve presentation skills you should take full advantage of the opportunity by using the individuals in the group wherever possible. This may mean getting some of them to run the exercises. It's important that you ensure the individuals are observed and debriefed by the rest of the group. By this simple observation, group members are able to see things that may or may not work for them. The more styles of presentation they see, the better.

Some of these exercises can be seen as very threatening to a few group members, so make sure you are prepared to offer your support and assistance if necessary.

M Mid-course energiser

Mid-course energisers can be used at any time you observe the group losing interest or falling asleep. Mid-course energisers are very similar in design to icebreakers, but they sometimes make the assumption that the members of the group know each other already. For this reason some of the exercises may appear a little threatening to some members of the group. If someone does not want to participate, let them sit back or act in an observer's role. You will normally find that they will join in as soon as they see how much fun the others are having.

These exercises are used to wake participants up, to get the blood moving, to keep participants from falling asleep after a lunch break, to simply get people back on line or to think about a new approach to a problem.

Experienced facilitators can also use these energisers to reduce tensions that may have built up with individuals or the group.

X Problem solving

Most of the problem-solving exercises have been designed to put participants, or small groups, in a situation where a solution is expected. These exercises are generally non-threatening.

The solutions that are given may not necessarily be the correct ones, so the facilitator must deal with this. The facilitator must also be aware that the solutions the individuals or groups put forward may actually be better ones than the facilitator originally had in mind.

Most of the problem-solving exercises also look at the use of synergy within the group. Synergy is where the total output of the group is more than the total combined output of the individuals.

All problem-solving exercises should be completely debriefed, so that everyone gets to hear other participants' ideas.

L Learning

These exercises are designed to let the participants see where their learning styles or attitudes need improvement. They tend to be more experimental in their application—that is, the participants are normally required to do something and come up with some kind of result or answer. After that phase of the exercise, the facilitator can normally draw out from the group better ways of doing the same thing with better results.

You must ensure that the whole exercise is totally debriefed and that every participant can see what the final results or methods should be. You should be aware that there are many different learning styles. Don't make the assumption that everyone in the group will learn the same way. Make certain you get plenty of feedback to check participant understanding.

P Perception

The perception exercises are generally fun for everyone to use. They are designed to see how participants perceive different situations or objects. The end result with most perception exercises is that participants are made aware of their need to use lateral thinking, to look at things in different ways, and to try to break down any preconceived stereotypes that they may be using.

As these exercises are fun to use, it is not uncommon to see them being used as icebreakers or mid-course energisers.

Some of the individuals in the group may have difficulty with perception exercises. If they do have difficulties, try to get the rest of the group to explain the different perceptions to them.

E Evaluation

Most of the evaluation exercises are designed so that participants can evaluate either themselves or the program. An important part of the evaluation process needs to be pointed out to the participants at the beginning of the exercise. This point is that any evaluation must be considered as constructive, not destructive. Things can be improved or rectified much more easily by using constructive evaluation. Destructive evaluation does nothing but leave some members with ill-feelings.

If any of these exercises are used for the purpose of program evaluation, it's a good idea to make sure the participants are told of the results, either verbally or in writing.

S Self-management

Exercises in the category of self-management allow the participants to find out where they can improve their own self-management techniques. These techniques are the same as time-management techniques, but with a different name. Here we look at improving participants' organisational skills.

Participants receive a lot of information and new ideas from other members within the group, so make sure that the whole group finds out what principles each participant used in the exercises.

Games Codes Grid

Game No.	Name	Page	Category	Icebreaker	Team building	Communication	Facilitator/presentation skills	Mid-course energiser	Problem solving	Learning	Perception	Evaluation	Self-management
1	Secret Sounds	17	ITMXP	●	●			●	●		●		
2	Numbers Game II	18	IMXLES	●				●	●	●		●	●
3	Score Three	21	TCFXLP		●	●	●		●	●	●		
4	POW	22	TCMX		●	●		●	●				
5	Mind Reader	24	IFMPS	●			●	●			●		●
6	Make It	27	TCLS		●	●				●			●
7	Characters	28	ITM	●	●			●					
8	Trivia Quest	29	ITMXLS	●	●			●	●	●			●
9	Floating Marbles	31	TCMX		●	●		●	●				
10	A Case of Doubles	32	ITMXPS	●	●			●	●		●		●
11	Dinner Guests	33	ITCM	●	●	●		●					
12	Share Market	34	IT	●	●								
13	Where Did It Go?	35	IMX	●				●	●				
14	Knots	38	ITMXS	●	●			●	●				●
15	Pig Test	39	IM	●				●					
16	Mixed Menu	40	ITFMXLP	●	●		●	●	●	●	●		
17	Shorthand	41	ITCMLPS	●	●	●		●		●	●		●
18	Rafts Ahoy!	42	TCXLS		●	●			●	●			●
19	Scrambled Eggs?	44	TCFMXLPES		●	●	●	●	●	●	●	●	●
20	Team Statue	46	ITC	●	●	●							
21	Jigsaws	47	ITCXS	●	●	●			●				●
22	Fruit Juice	48	TCMXL		●	●		●	●	●			
23	In My Experience...	49	IL	●						●			
24	Meeting Effectiveness	50	TCFXLPES		●	●	●		●	●	●	●	●
25	Training Rooms	52	TFMXLP		●		●	●	●	●	●		
26	Board Games	53	TCXLPS		●	●			●	●	●		●
27	That's Impossible	54	IMP	●				●			●		
28	Qwerty	55	TCMX		●	●		●	●				
29	Ready Mister Music	57	LPS							●	●		●
30	Opinions	58	LE							●		●	
31	Did I Say Cheek?	59	ICFMP	●		●	●	●			●		
32	Dial Tone	60	ICFPS	●		●	●				●		●

GAME NO.	NAME	PAGE	CATEGORY	Icebreaker	Team building	Communication	Facilitator/presentation skills	Mid-course energiser	Problem solving	Learning	Perception	Evaluation	Self-management
33	Pictures	62	CPS			•					•		•
34	Parking Lot	63	CES			•						•	•
35	Files Away	64	ITCMXL	•	•	•		•	•	•			
36	Last Resort	65	ITFMXLP	•	•		•	•	•	•	•		
37	Meeting Proposals	66	TCFXLPES		•	•	•		•	•	•	•	•
38	Service Secrets	68	TCMXLS		•	•		•	•	•			•
39	Ideas 'R' Us	72	ITMXL	•	•			•	•	•			
40	Doodleloo	75	IL	•						•			
41	All Scrambled Up	76	IMX	•				•	•				
42	Balloon Races	79	TX		•				•				
43	Add 'em Up	80	IMX	•				•	•				
44	Missing Matches	82	IMX	•				•	•				
45	Missing Numbers	84	IMX	•				•	•				
46	Centre of Operations	86	ITCFMXLPS	•	•	•	•	•	•	•	•		•
47	New Talent	87	ITM	•	•			•					
48	A to Z	88	ITCMXS	•	•	•		•	•				•
49	Who's Important?	90	ITMP	•	•			•			•		
50	Sacked or Promoted?	92	IMXLPS	•				•	•	•	•		•
51	Repeat After Me	94	CXLS			•			•	•			•
52	Name That Tune	96	IM	•				•					
53	Pyramid Puzzle	97	IMX	•				•	•				
54	External Limitations	99	LS							•			•
55	Good Sports	100	ITM	•	•			•					
56	What Did You See?	102	IFMXPS	•			•	•	•		•		•
57	Can't Lose!	104	TCMX		•	•		•	•				
58	XO Test	106	XLE						•	•		•	
59	Time-management Quiz	108	IPS	•							•		•
60	Mary's Lamb	110	ITCMS	•	•	•		•					•
61	Up or Down?	112	IMX	•				•	•				
62	Doug's Dog	114	IMXP	•				•	•		•		
63	Aliens	115	ITCMXLS	•	•	•		•	•	•			•
64	Planes Away	117	ITMXS	•	•			•	•				•
65	My Service Rules	120	IMPS	•				•			•		•
66	Mid-course Questionnaire	122	CMXLPE			•		•	•	•	•	•	
67	Most Valuable Things	124	XLE						•	•		•	

GAME NO.	NAME	PAGE	CATEGORY	Icebreaker	Team building	Communication	Facilitator/presentation skills	Mid-course energiser	Problem solving	Learning	Perception	Evaluation	Self-management
68	Daily Quiz	126	ITMXL	●	●			●	●	●			
69	Lottery Win	128	ITMXPS	●	●			●	●		●		●
70	Pre-course Interviews	130	ITFL	●	●		●			●			
71	Number Pyramid	132	IMX	●				●	●				
72	The Perfect Car	134	TCXP		●	●			●		●		
73	Team Theme	136	IT	●	●								
74	Shoe Shop	137	IMXP	●				●	●		●		
75	Minefield	138	TCMXS		●	●		●	●				●
76	Spring-clean	139	ITFMXLPS	●	●		●	●	●	●	●		●
77	Slash Equals What?	140	IMX	●				●	●				
78	Number Logic	142	TMX		●			●	●				
79	What Can I Sell You?	144	ICMXS	●		●		●	●				●
80	Reincarnation	146	ITM	●	●			●					
81	A Bag of Laughs	147	ITMS	●	●			●					●
82	Vacation Time	148	ITFMXLPS	●	●		●	●	●	●	●		●
83	Quick Review	149	MLE					●		●		●	
84	Line Up	150	ITM	●	●			●					
85	Magic Coins	151	ITMX	●	●			●	●				
86	Nicknames	152	I	●									
87	A Free Lunch	153	TCXLPS		●	●			●	●	●		●
88	Trivia Review	155	XLE					●	●			●	
89	Staff Turnover	156	TMXP		●			●	●		●		
90	Team Profile	157	TPS		●						●		●
91	Academy Awards	159	ME					●				●	
92	Problem-solving Cycle	161	TXLS		●				●	●			●
93	Popping Prizes	163	IM	●				●					
94	Guess Who I Saw?	164	I	●									
95	Sacred Cows	165	TCXPS		●	●			●		●		●
96	Up-selling	167	CXS			●			●				●
97	Letterman List	169	LE							●		●	
98	Bag Scavenger Hunt	170	ITMS	●	●			●					●
99	Line Up II	172	ITM	●	●			●					
100	Responses	173	LPES							●	●	●	●
101	Briefcase Clean Out	177	MXS					●	●				●
102	1 + 1	178	ITMX	●	●			●	●				
103	No-word Crossword	180	CFPS			●	●				●		●

1

Secret Sounds

ITMXP

TIME REQUIRED	SIZE OF GROUP	MATERIAL REQUIRED
1–2 minutes.	Unlimited.	A tape recorder and a number of prerecorded sounds. The sounds need to be things people would hear all the time. Examples might include turning on a light switch, a jug boiling, water running from a tap, a scanner operating or turning the page of a book. A prize will be required for each break; something easy like a packet of lollies.

Overview

An activity designed to get participants back on time after a break.

Goals

1. To have participants come back on time after a break.
2. To have some fun.

Procedure

1. Advise the group that they are going to have a break and that after the break there will be a contest.
2. Tell the group that at exactly _____ you are going to play a sound from the tape recorder and they will be required to guess what it is.
3. At the time stipulated, play the secret sound using the tape recorder.
4. The first person to guess what the sound is wins a prize. If no one guesses the correct answer the prizes can jackpot.

Discussion points

None.

Variations

1. Can be conducted as a small group exercise.
2. Noises from the participants' workplaces may be used.

TRAINER'S NOTES

The trainer may have to use a bit of licence when judging the answers.

2

Numbers Game II

TIME REQUIRED	SIZE OF GROUP	MATERIAL REQUIRED
5 minutes.	Unlimited.	Each participant will require a 'Numbers Game II' handout and a pen.

Overview

This activity can be used to show how 'practice makes perfect'.

Goals

1. To demonstrate how practice will give a better result.
2. To show how 'knowing a system' will give better results.

Procedure

1. Tell the group that they are going to participate in an experiment.
2. Give each person a copy of the 'Numbers Game II' handout and a pen. The handout should be given out face down. Ask the participants not to turn the handout over until they are told to.
3. Hold a copy of the handout up at the front of the class so everyone is looking at you. Tell them that the sheet is divided into two halves (top and bottom). Both halves are the same.
4. Now tell the group that when they turn their sheets over they are to use only the top part for this first bit of the exercise. When they look at the top of the sheet they will see that the number 1 is circled.
5. When asked, they are to pick up their pens and join number 1 to number 2, then number 2 to number 3 and so on.
6. They will have 30 seconds to join as many numbers as they can in the correct sequence. At the end of 30 seconds they will be asked to stop and

circle the number they are on. They are then to put their pens down.
7. After this has been completed ask the group if they can see a pattern with the numbers. Someone will notice that the numbers are set in 4 separate quadrants. The numbers go from top left to top right to bottom left to bottom right and then back again (like a star pattern). A prepared overhead transparency may demonstrate this better.
8. Now that they can see the pattern ask them to pick up their pens and go to the bottom part of their handout. They are now to join number 1 to number 2, then number 2 to number 3 and so on. They will again have 30 seconds to join as many numbers as they can in the correct sequence. At the end of 30 seconds they will be asked to stop and circle the number they are on.
9. After this has been completed ask the group if anyone didn't get a higher number the second time round. Few, if any, hands should go up. If they do just point out that some of the handouts may have had harder numbers to work with.

Discussion point

How does this exercise relate to what we are about to do? Answers should include understanding systems, practice gives better results, etc.

Variations

None.

TRAINER'S NOTES

A bit of 'trainer's licence' may be used with this exercise. The first 30 seconds may be cut short by a few seconds, while the next lot of 30 seconds may be extended by a few. This will give a far better result, meaning more people will have a higher number on the second phase of the exercise.

1 13 29 17 22 30 6
21 34 10
33 2 14 26 18
25
5 9
23 31 12 32 4
19 8 28
11 36
27
3 35 15 7 16 24 20

1 13 29 17 22 30 6
21 34 10
33 2 14 26 18
25
5 9
23 31 12 32 4
19 8 28
11 36
27
3 35 15 7 16 24 20

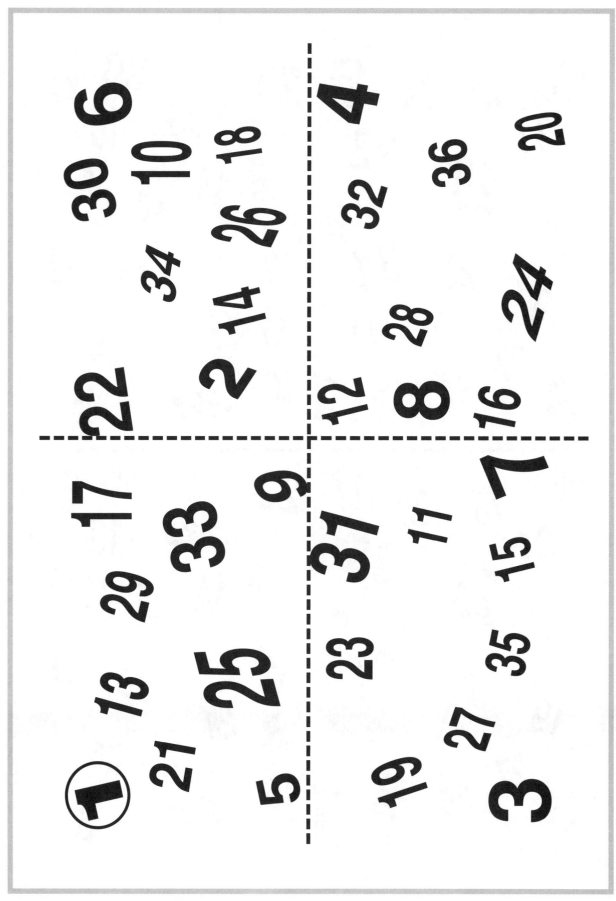

3

Score Three

TCFXLP

TIME REQUIRED	SIZE OF GROUP	MATERIAL REQUIRED
5–10 minutes.	Unlimited.	A box containing about forty pieces of screwed up paper. A waste bin is also required.

Overview

A quick activity to help participants see the benefit of using clear directions.

Goals

1. To demonstrate how good communication can improve results.
2. To develop a team spirit.

Procedure

1. Start this exercise by asking for a volunteer. Explain that the volunteer will be asked to follow a simple set of directions.
2. Once the volunteer has been selected ask them to come to the front of the room.
3. Place the volunteer at one side of the room and have them face the side wall. Place the bin behind them near the opposite wall making sure that the bin isn't directly behind them.
4. Hand the volunteer the box containing the pieces of screwed up paper.
5. Tell them that their job is to throw the pieces of screwed up paper over their shoulder and have them land in the waste bin. They are not allowed to turn around at any point to see how they are going. They must throw three pieces into the bin to be successful.

6. Advise the group that they will be able to give the person any verbal directions as appropriate to help them achieve the goal for example, 'more to the left'.
7. After the three pieces of paper have been thrown into the bin, ask your volunteer what helped to achieve the goal. Ask the group if it felt as though they had achieved the goal as well.

Discussion points

1. What helped the volunteer achieve the goal?
2. What hindered the volunteer?
3. Did the group feel as though they were part of a team?
4. How can we improve our instructions?
5. How does this apply in the workplace?

Variations

1. The screwed up pieces of paper can come from the sheets used in Game 70 in 100 Training Games.
2. Use two volunteers who are both blindfolded. One is throwing the pieces of paper and the other is holding the waste bin. Therefore, the group is giving them both verbal directions.

TRAINER'S NOTES

4

POW

TIME REQUIRED	SIZE OF GROUP	MATERIAL REQUIRED
2–3 minutes to introduce plus time to solve (this can vary dramatically between groups).	Unlimited, but will need to be broken into smaller groups of 4 people.	None. However, a prepared overhead of the 'POW' sheet could come in handy.

Overview

Here is an exercise to get everyone in the group thinking. It can be used for teamwork, communication or simply for fun.

Goals

1. To demonstrate the benefit of using a team to solve a problem.
2. To have some fun.
3. To give participants a problem to solve overnight on courses of longer duration.

Procedure

1. Introduce this activity by telling the group that they are going to be given a problem to solve.
2. Teams of 4 should be formed.
3. Ask the teams to imagine that they are being held prisoner in a POW camp and the camp commandant has asked them to stand in a particular sequence (shown on the POW sheet).
4. The first prisoner is standing behind a solid brick wall, facing away from it and wearing a red hat. The second prisoner is standing on the other side of the wall and facing the wall. He is wearing a blue hat. The third is standing behind the second, and facing him and the wall. He is wearing a red hat. The fourth prisoner is standing behind the third, again facing him and the wall. He has a blue hat on.
5. The prisoners are told that they are not allowed to move or turn around. They are not allowed to talk.
6. The commandant has given them a challenge. If one prisoner can tell the commandant what colour hat he is wearing he will let all 4 prisoners go. However, if the first answer is not correct

they will all be shot. They must remember that they are not allowed to talk, move or turn around. Therefore, the first answer given will determine their fate. They are told that there are 2 red hats and 2 blue hats.

7. Now ask the teams to tell you which prisoner can answer this problem correctly, and why.
8. After one team has solved the problem lead a discussion into the areas of teamwork, communication or problem solving.

Discussion points

1. Which prisoner can solve the problem, and why?
2. What helped the team solve this problem?
3. What hindered the team in solving this problem?
4. How does this affect us in the workplace?

Variations

1. The story can be modified to suit different groups.
2. Can be done individually, but may take a long time to process.
3. Can be given as a problem-solving activity for teams to work on overnight on longer courses.

Solution

Prisoner number 3 is the only one that can solve this problem. This prisoner can see that the person in front (prisoner number 2) is wearing a blue hat. Prisoner number 3 knows that if he is wearing a blue hat as well, the person behind him (prisoner number 4) would see the two blue hats and know that he had a red hat on. But as prisoner number 4 has said nothing, that means that he must be seeing both a red and a blue hat. Therefore, if prisoner number 3 can only see a blue hat in front, that means that he must have a red hat on.

TRAINER'S NOTES

POW

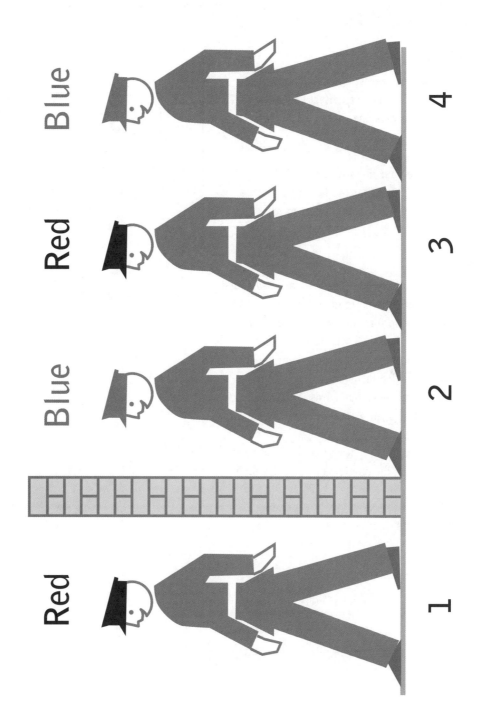

Red	Blue	Red	Blue
1	2	3	4

5

Mind Reader

TIME REQUIRED	SIZE OF GROUP	MATERIAL REQUIRED
2–5 minutes.	Unlimited.	A prepared 'Six Picture Cards' overhead and a prepared 'Six Minus One Picture Cards' overhead.

Overview

Here is a quick and interesting exercise to get the group thinking. It can be used effectively as an ice-breaker or a mid-course energiser.

Goals

1. To demonstrate your mind-reading abilities.
2. To introduce the fact that the facilitator isn't a mind reader and needs participants to ask questions.

Procedure

1. Start by telling the group that you have developed a new technique in mind reading.
2. Now tell the group that they will be shown an overhead displaying six cards from a deck of playing cards and that they are to mentally select one of the cards and focus on it. They are to totally ignore the other five cards. This is to be done in complete silence to allow their thoughts to be transferred.
4. Once this has been done, turn the overhead projector off and ask the participants to close their eyes for a few seconds and think of the card they have selected.
5. After several seconds tell the participants to open their eyes. Show them the second overhead with the five cards displayed and ask people to put their hand up if their card has been removed.
6. A quick set of instructions can now be given regarding the use of questions during the following training. This should highlight the fact that you have failed in your attempt to be able to mind read and that you really don't know what people are thinking.

Discussion points

1. How many people put their hand up without thinking why their card wasn't there?
2. How was this done?
3. Can we really read minds?
4. If you have any questions during the training—ask.

Variations

None.

TRAINER'S NOTES

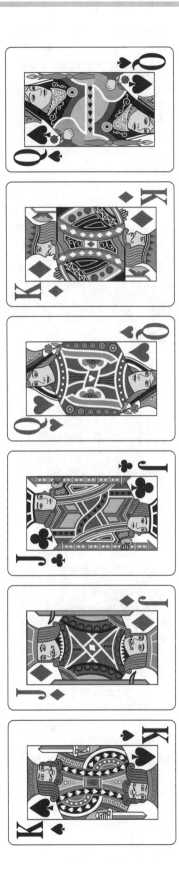

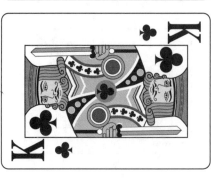

6

Make It

TCLS

TIME REQUIRED	SIZE OF GROUP	MATERIAL REQUIRED
20–30 minutes.	Up to 24, but will need to broken into groups of 5 to 7 people.	1 roll of sticky tape, 1 pair of scissors, 1 glue stick and as many pieces of paper, tinsel, streamers and the like that may be required.

Overview

An exercise designed to introduce negotiation skills.

Goals

1. To allow participants to use negotiation techniques in a controlled environment.
2. To see who the fastest thinkers in the group are.

Procedure

1. Break the group into smaller teams of 5 to 7 people.
2. Tell the group that each team is going to participate in the production of a collage and that there is a supply of materials scattered around the room for them to use during its construction.
3. Don't tell the participants that there is only 1 roll of sticky tape, 1 pair of scissors and 1 glue stick. The people who spot this fact first will be in a better position to negotiate.
4. Advise the teams that they have 15 minutes to construct their collage.

5. After the construction period everyone should become involved in the judging of each collage.
6. A discussion can now be led into the area of negotiation techniques.

Discussion points

1. Who had the best negotiating position? Why?
2. What negotiation techniques were used?
3. Did anyone use any other techniques such as stealing?
4. How did the teams feel when they realised that others had items that were necessary for them to use during construction?

Variations

1. Materials can be changed to things that might be more relevant to the group.
2. Only have a roll of sticky tape and do not use the scissors or the glue stick.

TRAINER'S NOTES

7

Characters

ITM

TIME REQUIRED	SIZE OF GROUP	MATERIAL REQUIRED
10–15 minutes depending on the size of the group.	Around 12 to 16 people.	None.

Overview

This an exercise where people can disclose information about themselves in a very non-threatening activity.

Goals

1. To find out a little about each participant in a non-threatening way.
2. For the facilitator/s to reveal a little more about themselves.

Procedure

1. Begin by introducing yourself and the course.
2. When the participant introductions have commenced each person should be asked the following question: 'If there were a movie made about your life, who would you pick to play your role, and why would you select that person?'.
3. Start by telling the group who you would select and why.

Discussion points

None.

Variation

May be done as a small group exercise if the initial group is too large.

TRAINER'S NOTES

8
Trivia Quest

ITMXLS

TIME REQUIRED	SIZE OF GROUP	MATERIAL REQUIRED
20–30 minutes depending on the size of the group.	Unlimited, but will need to be broken into smaller teams of 5 to 7 people.	A copy of the 'Trivia Quest' sheet as a handout for each group and a small prize for the winning team.

Overview

This is an activity that can be used at any time during training.

Goals

1. To get the groups working together as teams.
2. To develop an approach to problem solving.
3. To have some fun.

Procedure

1. Begin this exercise by informing the group that they will be involved in a trivia competition.
2. Ask the large group to break into smaller teams of 5 to 7 people.
3. Give each group a copy of the 'Trivia Quest' handout and tell them that they will have 15 minutes to answer as many of the 20 questions as possible. A prize will be awarded to the team that gets the most correct answers.
4. After the 15 minutes has elapsed tell the teams the correct answers and ask them to tally their scores. The winning team is then awarded their prize.
5. Lead a discussion into the areas of problem solving, or team work.

Discussion points

1. Which team got the highest number of correct answers?
2. What helped the teams get answers?
3. What stopped the teams getting answers?
4. What techniques did the teams use to get answers?
5. How does this apply in the workplace?

Variations

1. The 'Trivia Quest' handout can be used as an overhead instead.
2. Questions may be modified to suit the group.

Solution

1 = blue
2 = 'Days of our Lives'
3 = Eeyore
4 = 66
5 = 3
6 = Snidley Whiplash
7 = The height of the Nile River in full flood in 3400BC
8 = 148 800 000 kilometres or 93 000 000 miles
9 = MDCLXVI
10 = 12 756 kilometres or 7973 miles
11 = 8 640 000 (6000 per minute)
12 = 16
13 = **Resolution**
14 = Charles I
15 = Naomi James
16 = 2211
17 = 'Oh, my!'
18 = Love Me Tender
19 = A baker's shop in Pudding Lane
20 = rhythms

TRAINER'S NOTES

Trivia Quest

1. What colour was the Skipper's shirt on 'Gilligan's Island'?

2. What soap opera has an hourglass logo?

3. What is the donkey's name in **Winnie the Pooh**?

4. How many books are in the Bible (King James version)?

5. How many fingers do the Simpsons characters have?

6. Who was Dudley Doright's arch rival?

7. What was the earliest official statistic ever recorded?

8. How far is the sun from the earth?

9. What are the seven roman numerals?

10. What is the diameter of the earth at the equator?

11. Approximately how many lightning strikes are there every day around the world?

12. How many tablespoons are required to fill a standard cup?

13. What ship was Captain James Cook on when he reached Hawaii?

14. Who was the last English King to be executed?

15. Which New Zealand woman became the first woman to sail solo around the world in 1978?

16. What was Dirty Harry's badge number?

17. What were Captain Kirk's last words before he died?

18. What was Elvis Presley's first movie?

19. Where did the Great Fire of London break out in 1666?

20. What 7-letter word doesn't contain any of the 5 vowels?

9

Floating Marbles

TCMX

TIME REQUIRED	SIZE OF GROUP	MATERIAL REQUIRED
5 minutes.	Unlimited, but will need to be broken into groups of 5 to 7 people.	One cup and a marble for each group.

Overview

A quick problem-solving exercise used at the beginning of a training session to demonstrate the use of synergy.

Goals

1. To demonstrate the use of synergy.
2. To have some fun.
3. To energise the group.

Procedure

1. Break the large group into smaller groups of 5 to 7 people.
2. Give each team a cup and a marble.
3. Ask one member from each group to take the cup and place the marble inside it then walk from one side of the room to the other without allowing the marble to fall out of the cup.
4. After that has been completed, tell the participants that they now have to do the same thing again, but with the cup held upside down. The marble must remain inside the cup. They are not allowed to use any other materials for this exercise and have 2 minutes to work out a way of doing it.

5. After the 2 minutes has elapsed, ask each team to demonstrate their solution.
6. Prizes may be awarded to teams that solve the problem.

Discussion points

1. Why would it have been more difficult for individuals to solve this problem?
2. What helped the team come up with a solution?
3. What hindered the team from coming up with a solution?
4. How does this relate to the training we are about to become involved in?

Variation

If the teams are having difficulty solving the problem, you may want to 'stretch' the 2 minutes out a bit longer.

Solution

One possible solution is to put the marble in the cup and start spinning it. When the marble is spinning fast enough the cup may be turned upside down without the marble falling out. The spinning overcomes the pull of gravity.

TRAINER'S NOTES

31

10

A Case of Doubles

ITMXPS

TIME REQUIRED	SIZE OF GROUP	MATERIAL REQUIRED
2–10 minutes.	Unlimited.	A small prize for the winners.

Overview

A simple activity that can be used at any time during training.

Goals

1. To clear participants' minds before a coffee break.
2. To demonstrate the benefit of synergy if used as a small group exercise.
3. To have some fun.

Procedure

1. Advise the group that they are going to be given a simple problem to solve.
2. On a whiteboard write the following '?TTFFSS?'.
3. Ask the group to tell you what the two missing letters are. The person who gives the first correct answer will win a prize.
4. When the correct answer is given award a prize.

Discussion point

How does this relate to the training we are about to become involved in?

Discussion points, if used as a small group activity (see Variation section)

1. Why would it have been more difficult for individuals to solve this problem?
2. What helped the team come up with a solution?
3. What hindered the team from coming up with a solution?
4. How does this relate to the training we are about to become involved in?

Variation

Can be used as a small group exercise. Once the individual participants have been given approximately 20 seconds to look at the problem, ask them to break into smaller groups of 5 to 7 people. The small groups can now try and solve the problem. The first group to give the correct answer is given a group prize.

Solution

The 2 missing letters are 'O' and 'E'. Why? The sequence of letters is composed of the first letter of each number between 1 and 8. One Two Three Four Five Six Seven Eight.

TRAINER'S NOTES

Simple activities such as this one may be used after a coffee break. If participants are advised that there will be a game or quiz at the end of each break it will help to get them back on time, and ready for the next session (particularly if small prizes are awarded).

11

Dinner Guests

ITCM

TIME REQUIRED	SIZE OF GROUP	MATERIAL REQUIRED
10–15 minutes.	Unlimited.	A piece of paper and a pen for each participant.

Overview

An icebreaker to get the participants to identify their favourite characters or people they would like to be with.

Goals

1. To get the participants to identify people they respect.
2. To make the participants more aware of each other's perceptions.

Procedure

1. Ask the group to imagine that they are going to have a dinner party next Saturday night. They will be able to invite 3 famous people (either living or dead) to this imaginary dinner party. There will only be 4 people in attendance, yourself and the 3 guests. The guests can be politicians, actors, singers, religious leaders, royalty, business leaders, etc.
2. Hand out pens and paper and ask the participants to write down who they will invite.
3. After the list has been prepared each team member must tell the rest of the team their selection and the reasons behind their choices.

Discussion points

1. Did anyone have trouble trying to reduce their list to 3?
2. Did anyone have trouble not finding enough people to ask to dinner?

3. Now that the participants have heard the other selections would they like to change their list?

Variation

People within your organisation may be substituted for well-known personalities.

TRAINER'S NOTES

Share Market

IT

TIME REQUIRED	SIZE OF GROUP	MATERIAL REQUIRED
5–10 minutes at the start of each day.	Unlimited, but larger groups will need to be broken into smaller groups of 5 to 7 people.	Flipchart paper and pens for each group. Each group will also require a copy of today's newspaper showing the share market's results.

Overview

This activity can be used on courses of longer duration to promote team building.

Goals

1. To get small groups communicating.
2. To improve interaction between the participants.
3. To identify a common talking point for outside discussions.

Procedure

1. At the beginning of training ask the large group to form smaller teams of 5 to 7 people.
2. Give each team a sheet of flipchart paper, pens, and a copy of today's newspaper.
3. Tell them that each group has the task of investing $10 000 in the stock market and they have 5 minutes to look at yesterday's trading results in order to decide what shares to invest in.

4. Each morning the teams will be given 5 minutes to review their investments and work out what they are going to buy and sell.
5. All trades and balances are to be shown on their flipchart sheets for the other teams to look at. The cost of all transactions will be covered by the trainer, so they will not have to worry about brokers' fees, etc.
6. The team with the highest balance at the end of training will be declared the winner and awarded a small prize or certificate.

Discussion points

None.

Variation

Other rules may be applied, such as everything must be sold at the end of the trading day and different stocks must be purchased the following day, or each group must have a minimum portfolio of 10 companies, etc.

TRAINER'S NOTES

13

Where Did It Go?

IMX

TIME REQUIRED	SIZE OF GROUP	MATERIAL REQUIRED
2 minutes.	Unlimited.	A prepared set of cutouts (large enough for everyone to see when held up), or a prepared overhead.

Overview

A quick exercise that can be used before or after breaks.

Goals

1. To enable the participants to clear their heads.
2. To get people back on time after a coffee break.

Procedure

1. Advise the group that you are going to show them something that is quite amazing. It will be like magic.
2. Have a prepared set of cutouts laid out as shown in figure 1. These should be large enough for everyone to see (sticking them on a whiteboard makes it easier for everyone to see clearly what is happening).
3. Explain that what they can see is a total of 64 smaller squares (8 x 8).
4. Now rearrange the cutouts as shown in figure 2.
5. Ask the group how there can now be 65 squares using the same pieces.

Discussion points

1. Why was it difficult to see the solution?
2. How does this relate to what we are doing here?

Variation

May be done using a prepared overhead transparency if required (however the cutouts create a more 'magical' effect).

TRAINER'S NOTES

35

Where Did It Go?

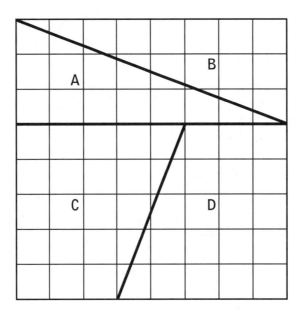

Figure 1

Where Did It Go?

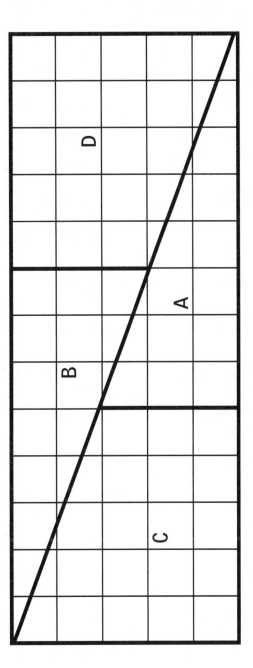

Figure 2

14

Knots

ITMXS

TIME REQUIRED	SIZE OF GROUP	MATERIAL REQUIRED
2–10 minutes.	Unlimited, but large groups will need to be broken into smaller groups of 5 to 7 participants.	A piece of rope for each group (about a metre long) and a small prize for the winners.

Overview

Another simple activity that can be used at any time during training.

Goals

1. To clear participants' minds before a coffee break.
2. To demonstrate the benefit of synergy if used as a small group exercise.
3. To have some fun.

Procedure

1. Advise the group that they are going to be given a simple problem to solve.
2. Break the large group into smaller groups of 5 to 7 participants.
3. Hand each group a piece of rope.
4. Tell the group that there is an old legend about an ancient magician who could tie a knot in a piece of rope while holding on to both ends of it. Their job is to work out how this was done.

5. Award a prize to the group who gives the correct answer.

Discussion points

1. Why would it have been more difficult for individuals to solve this problem?
2. What helped the team come up with a solution?
3. What hindered the team from coming up with a solution?
4. How does this relate to the training we are about to become involved in?

Variations

None.

Solution

Have one person fold their arms. Then give them the free ends of the rope in each hand. As they unfold their arms the rope will automatically knot itself.

TRAINER'S NOTES

15

Pig Test

TIME REQUIRED	SIZE OF GROUP	MATERIAL REQUIRED
5 minutes.	Unlimited.	A piece of paper and a marking pen for each participant.

Overview

Here is a fun icebreaker or an activity that can be used to add a bit of humour to your training.

Goal

To have some fun.

Procedure

1. Give each person a sheet of paper and a pen and tell them to draw a pig.
2. After everyone has finished drawing their pig ask them to listen to the following information (it may be used as a script if necessary).
3. The pig serves as a useful test of the personality traits of the drawer. If the pig is drawn:
   - towards the top of the paper, you are positive and optimistic
   - towards the middle, you are a realist
   - towards the bottom, you are pessimistic and have a tendency to behave negatively
   - facing left, you believe in tradition, are friendly, and remember dates (birthdays, etc.)
   - facing right, you are innovative and active, but don't have a strong sense of family, nor do you remember dates
   - facing front on (looking at you), you are direct, enjoy playing devil's advocate and neither fear nor avoid discussions
   - with many details, you are analytical, cautious, and distrustful
   - with few details, you are emotional, you care little for details and are a risk taker
   - with fewer than 4 legs showing, you are insecure or are living through a period of major change
   - with 4 legs showing, you are secure, stubborn, and stick to your ideals
   - if there are more than 4 legs, you are stupid
   - the size of the ears indicates how good a listener you are—the bigger the better
   - 'Who didn't draw a tail on their pig?' The length of the tail indicates the quality of your sex life—again more is better
   - 'OK, so who had the longest tail?'
4. You may wish to have all the participants stick their drawings on a wall as a display during training. If this is done they can be referred to humorously during the training session.

Discussion points

None.

Variations

1. The analysis can be trimmed down if required to save time.
2. This can be done very effectively as a PowerPoint® type presentation.

Source

Adapted from a game suggested by Barb De Corti, Western Australia

---

TRAINER'S NOTES

16

Mixed Menu

ITFMXLP

TIME REQUIRED	SIZE OF GROUP	MATERIAL REQUIRED
20–30 minutes.	Unlimited.	Each team may require a sheet of flipchart paper and pens.

Overview

This is a team-building activity that may be used at any time during training.

Goal

To develop a team approach to problem solving.

Procedure

1. Advise the group that they are going to be given a task to complete. The large group may be broken into smaller teams if necessary, but if the large group is to work as one team after the training it may be worthwhile keeping them together.
2. Tell them that the CEO of the company has just decided to diversify from the core business of the company and open a chain of restaurants.
3. Each team has been given the job of designing a 'perfect' restaurant menu. This task is to be completed in 10 minutes.
4. At the end of the 10 minutes one person (from each team) is to give a presentation of the final design.

Discussion points

1. How did the team arrive at a consensus in the time frame allocated?
2. How were any differences resolved?
3. How does this exercise apply in the workplace?

Variation

Other activities can be used rather than designing a menu.

TRAINER'S NOTES

If all the participants are from the same company they can be told that this is a directive from their current CEO in step 2 of the procedure. If the participants are from a number of different companies they should be told that they have all been employed in a new company and that this is a directive from their new CEO.

17
Shorthand

TIME REQUIRED	SIZE OF GROUP	MATERIAL REQUIRED
15–20 minutes.	Unlimited, but large groups will need to be broken into smaller groups of 5 to 7 participants.	A current newspaper, writing paper and pens for each group.

Overview

This activity can be used at any time during training to get a group working as a team.

Goals

1. To improve teamwork.
2. To improve time-management skills by using a skimming technique.

Procedure

1. Ask the large group to form smaller groups of 5 to 7 people.
2. After the groups have formed give each team a copy of a current newspaper, sheets of blank writing paper and some pens.
3. Tell them that they have been employed as 'shorthand journalists'. Their task is to summarise the major stories in their newspaper to less than 10 lines of written text.
4. At the end of 10 minutes each team is to give a quick summary of each of their summaries.
5. The team with the most concise report may be awarded a small prize.

Discussion points

1. What helped the group select the most important items?
2. What problems did each team have in selecting the items?
3. How difficult, or easy, was it is to select the items?
4. Who had the best ideas, and what were they?
5. How does this apply to what we currently do or don't do?

Variations

1. Each team may be asked to summarise the 10 items they feel are the most trivial.
2. Flipchart paper may be used instead of writing paper.

TRAINER'S NOTES

18

Rafts Ahoy!

TCXLS

TIME REQUIRED	SIZE OF GROUP	MATERIAL REQUIRED
1½–2 hours.	Unlimited, but large groups will need to be broken into smaller groups of 4 or 5 people.	1 swimming pool. Each team will also require 6 medium-size cardboard boxes, one marking pen and 1 roll of masking tape or a small roll of gaffer tape. The boxes can be obtained from your local grocery store or bottle shop.

Overview

This is an activity that's strictly for outdoor use, but unlike a lot of outdoor games it's inexpensive.

Goals

1. To develop teamwork.
2. To demonstrate the benefit of synergy.
3. To energise the group.

Procedure

1. Break the large group into smaller groups of 4 to 5 people. The teams need to be broken up so that there is an even spread of large and small people in each group.
2. Each team is now given 6 medium-size cardboard boxes and a small roll of gaffer tape.
3. Take everyone out to the side of the swimming pool.
4. Tell them that the activity is in two phases.
5. Phase one of the task is to construct a raft, using only the materials provided. One hour will be allowed for this part of the exercise.
6. During phase one the team is also required to name their raft.
7. At the end of phase one all teams and their rafts should be lined up at the edge of the pool ready for phase two.

8. Phase two is the testing phase. To pass the test, the raft must be able to float across the pool carrying one of the team members—and not sink! The raftsperson is not allowed to enlist the help of any other team members or substitutes.
9. A vote should be carried out at the end to see which team had the best vessel. A prize or certificate should be awarded.

Discussion points

1. Which team created the best raft?
2. What helped the team with this exercise?
3. What problems were encountered?
4. What roles did people assume?
5. Did any leaders emerge?
6. Was there any conflict? If so, how was it resolved?
7. What does this exercise demonstrate?

Variations

1. An interesting variation is to make this a truly competitive exercise. During the briefing, tell each team that the test in phase two will include a race. The first team to cross the pool (using a Le Mans style start) will be declared the winner.
2. The attached 'Rafts Ahoy' handout may be used with the initial team briefing.

TRAINER'S NOTES

If the teams are finding this activity too hard you may, at your discretion, give out additional resources to all groups (such as plastic garbage bags) during phase one. Additionally the time limit for phase one may be extended.

Rafts Ahoy!

Your team represents a company that designs, builds and tests custom-made rafts.

For this exercise you will have 60 minutes to design and construct your raft. During this part of the exercise you are also required to decide on a name for your vessel. On completion of this phase your raft will be evaluated and put through a test. To pass the test your raft must be able to sail across the pool carrying one of your team members. Your raftsperson is not allowed to enlist the help of any other team members or substitutes.

One final point—the raft must not sink!

Good luck and happy sailing.

19

Scrambled Eggs?

TCFMXLPES

TIME REQUIRED	SIZE OF GROUP	MATERIAL REQUIRED
75–90 minutes.	Unlimited, but will need to be broken into smaller teams of 5 to 7 people.	One raw egg for each small group, a small roll of sticky tape for each group, 10 drinking straws, 3 elastic bands, a pair of scissors, 4 metres of string, an A4 size sheet of paper, and a set of coloured marking pens. Spare eggs are advisable. A briefing sheet is included should you wish to distribute it to the groups.

Overview

This exercise is designed to involve participants in a number of issues such as problem solving, team building, teamwork and customer service skills.

Goals

1. To allow participants to identify some strategies in customer service.
2. To allow participants to practise some problem-solving techniques.

Procedure

1. Ask the participants to break into small groups of 5 to 7 people.
2. Tell the groups that they represent companies that produce spacecraft. These companies will be competing for a lucrative contract to construct a particular type of craft for the next decade.
3. Each group has the task of designing, constructing and evaluating a spacecraft suitable for the transportation of raw eggs. They will have 45 minutes to design and construct their Egg Transportation Device (ETD) using the material supplied.
4. Explain to the groups that at the end of the construction phase there will be an evaluation. The ETDs are to be launched a minimum of 4 metres into the air. (This is achieved by having the team throw the ETD into the air.) The egg must not break during this 'test flight'. Should the egg

break during the flight the company will be sued for damages.
5. The teams who pass the test flight should now vote on the best design. The winning team should be given an award.
6. When the evaluation phase is completed a discussion may be led into problem-solving strategies, teamwork, customer service skills, etc.

Discussion points

1. Which teams passed the evaluation criterion?
2. Were there any problems? How were they broken down? Who did what?
3. Did any team decide to create a joint venture with another team? Why or why not?
4. What was assumed by the teams? (See Game 35 in 101 More Training Games.)
5. Did any group ask the customer for more specific details such as the required colour, company logos and the like? Why? Why not?
6. Did any group get the customer involved in the process? Why? Why not?

Variations

1. Sticks may be used instead of straws.
2. Boiled eggs may be used to save cleaning up if any breakages occur.
3. Different coloured straws and pens can be given to each group.
4. Materials may be unevenly distributed among the groups.

TRAINER'S NOTES

Scrambled Eggs?

Your team represents a company that designs, builds and flies custom-made spacecraft. You will be competing for a lucrative contract to design and construct Egg Transportation Devices (ETDs) for the next decade.

For this exercise you will have 45 minutes to design and construct your ETD. You may use only the materials provided for this exercise which include:

one raw egg
1 small roll of sticky tape
10 drinking straws
3 elastic bands
1 pair of scissors
4 metres of string
1 sheet of A4 size paper
1 set of coloured marking pens.

On completing the design and construction of your ETD it will be evaluated and put through a 'test flight'. The ETDs are to be launched a minimum of 4 metres into the air. (This is achieved by having the team throw the ETD into the air.) The egg must not break during this test flight. Should the egg break, the company will be sued for damages.

All the raw materials (pun definitely intended) will be distributed by your customer.

Good luck!

20

Team Statue

ITC

TIME REQUIRED	SIZE OF GROUP	MATERIAL REQUIRED
15–20 minutes.	Unlimited, but large groups will need to be broken into smaller groups of 5 to 7 participants.	One bag of modelling clay for each group (and plenty of handtowels).

Overview

An activity to allow groups to form an initial bond.

Goals

1. To have an identifier for each small group.
2. To encourage communication.
3. To allow individuals in each group to bond.
4. To have fun!

Procedure

1. Divide the group into smaller groups of 5 to 7 members.
2. Give each group a bag of modelling clay.
3. Tell them that they now have 10 minutes to create a sculpture that reflects a team theme.
4. After the 10 minutes has elapsed, let each group display their creation and explain what it is and what it means.
5. The team with the most creative design may be awarded a small prize.
6. Place the sculptures around the room for display during the training.

Discussion points

1. What were the themes?
2. Did everyone quickly agree with the theme?
3. How does this activity affect the remaining time for each group here in training?

Variation

Some group members may be rotated during the exercise.

TRAINER'S NOTES

21

Jigsaws

ITCXS

TIME REQUIRED	SIZE OF GROUP	MATERIAL REQUIRED
10–20 minutes.	Unlimited, but large groups will need to be broken into smaller groups of 4.	Each group will require a jigsaw puzzle (50 to 100 pieces). Each puzzle will be broken up and split into 4 lots. Each lot will be placed in a paper bag (1 for each participant).

Overview

This activity is designed to improve teamwork and communication within workgroups.

Goals

1. To demonstrate how improved communication can improve the quality of work.
2. To demonstrate how essential good communication is for improved teamwork.

Procedure

1. Start by advising the group that they will be involved in a team exercise.
2. Ask the participants to form groups of 4. Any odd numbers should be worked into groups of 3, and the bags set up to suit the smaller groups.
3. Give each person a bag containing parts of the team jigsaw.
4. Tell the participants that they have all the parts of a jigsaw between them. They will have 3 minutes for the first part of this exercise. They are to put all the parts down in front of them. They are only allowed to move their own parts and this must be done in silence.

5. After the 3 minutes have elapsed advise the participants that they can now talk and also move other team members' pieces.
6. After the groups have completed their jigsaws lead into a discussion on communication, trust and teamwork.

Discussion points

1. Why was it difficult to start the exercise?
2. Why was it easier and faster when participants were allowed to talk?
3. How does this apply in the workplace?
4. How can we improve the results back in our own workplace based on what we've just seen?

Variations

1. Give each group the same puzzle and make it a competition.
2. Make your own jigsaw puzzles using written messages rather than pictures.

TRAINER'S NOTES

Use different coloured bags for each group to ensure the bags don't get mixed up. Mark the back of each piece with a number so that, should pieces get mixed up, they can be sorted easily for reuse.

22

Fruit Juice

TIME REQUIRED	SIZE OF GROUP	MATERIAL REQUIRED
5 minutes.	Unlimited, but will need to be broken into groups of 5 to 7 people.	A small prize for the winning team. Containers and liquid may also be needed.

Overview

Here is a simple problem for teams to work out.

Goals

1. To energise the group.
2. To demonstrate the use of synergy.
3. To have some fun.

Procedure

1. Break the large group into smaller groups of 5 to 7 people.
2. Tell each team that you will be giving them a problem to solve. The first team to give a correct answer will win a prize.
3. Here is the problem. You are to split some orange juice into three equal portions. The juice comes in a 240 mL container. You only have three other containers to use, each holding 50 mL, 110 mL, and 130 mL respectively. How can you divide the orange juice into three equal portions? If the participants need a hint, tell them that it will take at least four steps.
4. The first team with a correct answer should be awarded their prize.

Discussion points

1. What helped the team come up with a solution?
2. What hindered the team from coming up with a solution?
3. How does this relate to the training we are currently involved in?

Variations

1. Each group can be given actual containers and juice (or water) to use.
2. For groups that really need to be challenged, this can be done as a blindfolded exercise.

Solution

Here is one of several possible solutions:

Vessel size	240 mL	130 mL	110 mL	50 mL
To start	240	0	0	0
First	80	0	110	50
Second	80	130	30	0
Third	80	80	30	50
Fourth	80	80	80	0

TRAINER'S NOTES

In My Experience ...

TIME REQUIRED	SIZE OF GROUP	MATERIAL REQUIRED
2–5 minutes.	Unlimited.	A whiteboard or flipchart.

Overview

A simple activity to be used at the start of training to show how much experience everyone has.

Goals

1. To identify how much experience everyone has.
2. To show that the facilitator isn't the only one with the answers.

Procedure

1. At the beginning of training, point out that the participants in the training room have loads of experience in the topic area.
2. Ask everyone to think about the topic and total the amount of experience (in years) that they have in this area. The topics for this activity can range from supervision skills, to training skills, to cooking skills, to operating machines, to reading skills, etc.
3. Go round the group and ask each person to say how much experience they have. These figures should be written on the whiteboard as they are given.
4. When all the figures are written up they should be totalled.
5. Summarise by saying that the group has a vast amount of experience between them, and this experience should be shared as they go through the program.

Discussion points

1. Did everyone recognise that they already had some experience in the area?
2. Are we able to learn from each other's experiences?

Variation

Have everyone come up to the board and write the information themselves. You can then total the numbers as they are written.

TRAINER'S NOTES

24

Meeting Effectiveness

TIME REQUIRED	SIZE OF GROUP	MATERIAL REQUIRED
30–60 minutes.	Up to 24, but will need to be broken down into smaller groups of 5 to 7 people.	One copy of the 'Meeting Effectiveness' handout for each person and a pen.

Overview

If you have to do some training on meetings here is a questionnaire that may help the participants gain some valuable information.

Goals

1. To identify how effectively meetings are being conducted.
2. To find ways of making meetings run more effectively.

Procedure

1. Ask the large group to break into smaller groups of 5 to 7 people.
2. Give each person a copy of the 'Meeting Effectiveness' handout.
3. Advise the groups that they are going to be involved in a reflective exercise. They are to think about meetings they have been involved with recently and answer the questions shown on their handout. They will have 10 minutes to do this.
4. After the handouts have been completed, ask each of the small groups to discuss their individual responses together and identify 10 ways to make meetings run more effectively.
5. Each group should then give a short presentation on their 10 points.

Discussion points

1. How can you make sure you follow these rules after today?
2. Why aren't these things being done at present?

Variation

Have all the small groups reach a consensus on the 'Top 10' rules after all the groups have given their feedback.

TRAINER'S NOTES

Meeting Effectiveness

1. How satisfied are you about your contribution at meetings?

_____

_____

2. How would you describe the way your team makes decisions in meetings?

_____

_____

3. How well does your team solve problems in meetings?

_____

_____

4. How effectively do your team members work together in meetings?

_____

_____

5. How effectively does the leader manage meetings?

_____

_____

6. What could be done to improve the effectiveness of your meetings?

_____

_____

7. What could you do to make this team more effective with its meetings?

_____

_____

Training Rooms

TFMXLP

TIME REQUIRED	SIZE OF GROUP	MATERIAL REQUIRED
30–40 minutes.	Unlimited, but large groups will need to be broken into smaller groups of 5 to 7 people.	Each team will require a sheet of flipchart paper and pens. They will also need some cardboard, scissors and a ruler.

Overview

A team-building activity that may be used at any time during training.

Goal

To develop a team approach to problem solving.

Procedure

1. Advise the group that they are going to be given a task to complete.
2. Break the large group into smaller groups of 5 to 7 people.
3. Tell them that the training manager of the company has decided to do a complete refit of the training room/s and they have been given the job of redesigning this area.
4. Advise the teams that they have 45 minutes to design a scaled diagram of the training room with movable representations of the furnishings. The model must be of a sufficient standard to enable the training manager to experiment with different layouts.

5. At the end of the 45 minutes each team should give a short presentation on its design and explain the approach adopted in completing the task.
6. The team delivering the best design may be awarded a prize or certificate.

Discussion points

1. How did the team arrive at a consensus in the time frame allocated?
2. How were any differences resolved?
3. What assumptions were made?
4. Did everyone use the same jargon (e.g. metric versus imperial)?
5. Did anyone check with the customer (or other customers) about what was required?
6. What role did everyone take?
7. Did any leaders emerge?
8. How does this exercise apply in the workplace?

Variation

Other items may be built such as a holiday resort.

TRAINER'S NOTES

Board Games

TCXLPS

TIME REQUIRED	SIZE OF GROUP	MATERIAL REQUIRED
1½–2 hours.	Up to 24, but larger groups will need to be broken into teams of 5 to 7 people.	Each team will require sheets of coloured board, scissors, coloured marking pens, rulers, sticky tape, and anything else you can get your hands on.

Overview

This is a more complex game that requires all participants to become involved in a team activity.

Goals

1. To show the benefits of team members working together.
2. To allow participants to be more creative.
3. To develop a team approach to problem solving.
4. To improve time-management skills.

Procedure

1. Break the large group into smaller groups of 5 to 7 people.
2. Hand out all the resources listed above to the teams.
3. Tell the teams that they are going to be given an amazing opportunity. Since last Christmas all the retail stores have been short on board games for adults. If they can come up with a good idea they may be able to make a fortune!
4. Inform the teams that they have 60 minutes to design a new board game for adult use only. If they require any other resources (hopefully they will) they are responsible for finding them.
5. At the end of the specified time frame ask each team to give a presentation on their game (what it is, how they designed it, what it's called, how it's played, what the rules are, how to win, etc.)

6. Once the presentations have been completed the large group should vote on which team has the best game.

Discussion points

1. Were there any problems? How were they broken down? Who did what?
2. How did the team arrive at a consensus within the time frame allocated?
3. How were any differences resolved?
4. Did any leaders emerge?
5. What time-management problems were identified?
6. Did any group approach other customers and ask for their opinion? Why? Why not?
7. How can these ideas be applied back in the workplace or here in training?

Variations

1. Rather than the board game for adults, one could be designed for children aged between 12 and 16.
2. For training courses of a longer duration this could be an evening exercise for the teams to work on in their own time.
3. You may tell the teams what the name of the game is going to be, for example, Top Gun, Venus, Chained Inn, Titanic, Tonight's the Night, etc.

TRAINER'S NOTES

27

That's Impossible

TIME REQUIRED	SIZE OF GROUP	MATERIAL REQUIRED
1–2 minutes.	Unlimited.	None.

Overview

This is a very quick icebreaker that can be used to lighten up a training session.

Goal

To allow participants to laugh at themselves.

Procedure

1. At the beginning of training tell the group that you are going to start off by giving them a test. The test is simply titled, 'Do I Really Have To Be Here?'. If they can pass the test they may be excused for the rest of the course.
2. Tell the participants to place one of their hands on the desk in front of them with all of their fingers spread out.
3. Ask them to tilt their hand up slightly at the back (near the wrist) and tuck their middle finger underneath as far as they can. Now they are to place their hand down as flat as they can on the table, keeping the middle finger tucked under.
4. Next, ask them if it's possible that they may learn something new during their training. It they think it is, ask them to raise their thumb off the table. They can now put their thumb back down.
5. Now ask everyone if they are looking forward to finishing on time this afternoon. If they are they

should raise their pinkie (or little finger). They can now put their pinkie back down.
6. Ask the participants if they would like to have a break during the training session. If they would they should raise their pointer (or index finger).
7. With all of their fingers back in the original position (with the middle finger still tucked underneath), finally ask them if they would rather go home than sit here. If they would they should raise their ring finger.
8. If everyone has their hand in the correct position, it is almost impossible to lift the appointed finger off the table. If anyone does, just tell that it wasn't lifted high enough and lacked the necessary enthusiasm. Therefore, they had better stay here.
9. After the laughter, let everyone know you are pleased that they would rather spend their day with you.

Discussion points

None.

Variation

All questions can be modified to suit the group and the training topic.

TRAINER'S NOTES

28

Qwerty

TCMX

TIME REQUIRED	SIZE OF GROUP	MATERIAL REQUIRED
20–30 minutes.	Unlimited, but a large group will need to be broken into smaller groups of 5 to 7 people.	A prepared 'Common Keys' overhead.

Overview

This activity can be used to improve teamwork and encourage the sharing of ideas.

Goals

1. To improve teamwork.
2. To encourage participants to share ideas.
3. To identify some reasons why people find it difficult to change their ways.

Procedure

1. Break the larger group into smaller groups of 5 to 7 people.
2. Tell the groups that their company is going to replace all of its computers. The new computers are going to be custom made and, as a result, the participants will be able to have whatever they want on the new machines.
3. Advise each team that their task is to design a new layout for their computer keyboard. They have 10 minutes to design the key layout and draw it to show to the other groups.
4. Let the teams know that research has been done and it would appear that there are some keyboard keys used more than others. This information will be useful in their design. Show them the 'Common Keys' overhead.
5. After the winning team has been chosen and the awards made, lead into a discussion on change and why there is so much resistance to it. The questions shown in the discussion points below will help participants focus on the topic.

Discussion points

1. Even with these very practical designs why is it that most people wouldn't use them? (List comments on a whiteboard.)
2. How can we get people to accept change more readily?
3. How can you implement change based on what you will learn during this training?

Variations

None.

TRAINER'S NOTES

Common Keys

Current research indicates that, in this company, the frequency of use for each of the keys on the keyboard is as follows:

A	N		P	` '		' X	V
O	S		Y	< ,		Q	B	Z
E	T		F	> .		J	M	Shift
U	=		G	? /		K	W	
70%			**22%**			**8%**	

70% — A, N, O, S, E, T, U, =

22% — P, ` ' , Y, < , , F, > . , G, ? /

8% — ' X, V, Q, B, Z, J, M, Shift, K, W

Ready Mister Music

LPS

TIME REQUIRED	SIZE OF GROUP	MATERIAL REQUIRED
None.	Unlimited.	A CD player and an appropriate CD.

Overview

This activity will encourage the group to get back together after breaks or small group activities.

Goal

To get the group back together after small group activities, coffee breaks or lunch.

Procedure

1. At the beginning of the training session let the group know that there will some group activities and several breaks during the day.
2. Also let them know that it is important that they come back on time after these activities or breaks and that it is sometimes very easy to lose track of time if an activity is particularly engrossing.
3. Tell them that you are going to help them to regroup on time. Whenever it is necessary for the group to resume training you are going to play a particular track on your CD player (play the track now).
4. Next time you have a break or finish a small group activity, just play the tune (with plenty of volume)—you'll be surprised at the effectiveness of this technique.

Discussion points

None.

Variation

If a CD player is not available there are alternative things to use, for example, a whistle, a bell, or a pocket alarm (they all work equally as well).

TRAINER'S NOTES

Use a motivational type track or something that suggests a sense of urgency (I like to use 'Move Baby Move').

30

Opinions

TIME REQUIRED	SIZE OF GROUP	MATERIAL REQUIRED
10–15 minutes.	Unlimited, but more sheets will be required for larger groups.	Prepared flipcharts and lots of marking pens. One flipchart should be titled, 'The most valuable thing I got from this training was...' and the other should be titled, 'These are the suggestions I would make for future programs'.

Overview

This exercise should be used at the conclusion of training to see what people have learned.

Goals

1. To gain feedback from participants on what they perceived to be the most valuable parts of the training.
2. To gain feedback from participants on how to improve future training in this area.

Procedure

1. At the conclusion of training let the participants know that you would like some constructive comments about the training they have just been through.
2. Point out the 2 flipcharts and read the title on each page.
3. Tell the group that you will be leaving the room for a few minutes and they are free to write whatever they want on the sheets while you are gone.

4. Ask everyone to stand up, move to the charts, and grab a marking pen (if you don't do this you won't get much feedback).
5. When you come back thank the group. After everyone leaves summarise the comments and pass the information on to the appropriate people.

Discussion points

None.

Variations

1. A tape recorder may be left in the room instead of having people write things on the charts.
2. Participants may be encouraged to write their comments on a piece of paper. After they have completed this, the paper can be placed in a box.

TRAINER'S NOTES

Did I Say Cheek?

ICFMP

TIME REQUIRED	SIZE OF GROUP	MATERIAL REQUIRED
1 minute.	Unlimited.	None.

Overview

A simple activity to demonstrate the power of non-verbal communication.

Goals

To demonstrate how powerful nonverbal communication can be.

Procedure

1. Ask the group to put their pens and other materials down and look at you.
2. When everyone is looking directly at you, ask them all to put their closed fist on their cheek. Demonstrate this at exactly the same time as you say it but put your fist on your chin rather than your cheek.
3. As soon as everyone has done this, tell them that their hand is now superglued into place and cannot be moved.
4. Have the participants look around and see how many people actually followed your verbal instruction. Half of the group will have their hand on their cheek, the other half on their chin.
5. Lead into a discussion on verbal and nonverbal communication.

Discussion points

1. Why did some people follow the visual cue as opposed to the verbal communication?
2. How many people actually went to put their hand on their chin, but realised before they did it that the verbal request was different and followed that instead?

Variation

This exercise should be followed by Game 32.

TRAINER'S NOTES

Dial Tone

ICFPS

TIME REQUIRED	SIZE OF GROUP	MATERIAL REQUIRED
2–5 minutes.	Unlimited.	A prepared 'Dial Tone' overhead.

Overview

Here are some statistics that trainers sometimes find useful to present in their training sessions. They are good for communications or customer service training, as well as presentation skills, etc.

Goals

To show the importance of nonverbal communication.

Procedure

1. During training (especially any discussions on communication) show the 'Dial Tone' overhead.
2. Explain to the group that what they say to people is only a very small part of the message they convey. What they communicate through their body language and the tone of their voice is just as important as the words they use.

Discussion points

1. How can we communicate more effectively knowing this information?
2. Can the group think of any examples?

Variation

This exercise works best if preceded by Game 31.

TRAINER'S NOTES

Dial Tone

Communication—face to face

55% of our communication is through our body language

38% of our communication is through the tone of our voice

7% of our communication is through the words we use

Communication—on the phone

82% of our communication is through the tone of our voice

18% of our communication is through the words we use

33
Pictures

TIME REQUIRED	SIZE OF GROUP	MATERIAL REQUIRED
10–15 minutes.	Unlimited, but large groups will need to be broken into smaller groups of 3 or 4 people.	Numerous pictures of people cut from newspapers and magazines. The people should not be well known and should come from a wide range of backgrounds, professions, and nationalities. It would be useful to select photographs that don't obviously reflect the person's profession or background.

Overview

Even after all these years of education people still use stereotypes. Here is an exercise to prove this point.

Goal

To demonstrate how people stereotype.

Procedure

1. Break the large group into smaller groups of 3 or 4 people.
2. Hand each group 6 of the photographs and tell them they have 5 minutes to work out as much as they can about each person, based purely on what they can see in the picture.
3. Ask each group to give a very quick presentation on their photographs and their assumptions. If any background is known about these people you may offer this in conclusion. You may find it useful with large groups to have the photographs printed on overheads so that the whole group can see them.
4. After the presentations lead into a discussion on stereotyping.

Discussion points

1. Why did some people have preconceived ideas about the people shown in the photographs?
2. How does this affect us in the workplace?

Variation

If the photographs are printed on overheads they can be shown to the group one at a time. That way you can just ask for comments and feedback.

TRAINER'S NOTES

34

Parking Lot

CES

TIME REQUIRED	SIZE OF GROUP	MATERIAL REQUIRED
None.	Unlimited.	Flip chart and pen.

Overview

This activity is designed to deal with questions that pop up during training and need to be put 'on hold' to be discussed at the end of the session (if time permits).

Goal

To ensure questions aren't forgotten and can be put on hold to be dealt with later if time permits.

Procedure

1. Get a clean sheet of flipchart paper and label it 'Parking Lot'.
2. If there are any questions asked by participants that are relevant, or almost relevant, to the topic but which may take too long to answer, tell the questioner that you are going to put their ques-

tion in your Parking Lot. This will ensure that it won't be forgotten and can be addressed at the end of the session, if time permits.
3. Write the question on the sheet and move on.
4. If questions are put into the Parking Lot during training, try to ensure there is either enough time to deal with them at the end of the session or that participants are directed to where answers can be found.

Discussion points

None.

Variation

A section of the whiteboard can be marked off as the Parking Lot instead of using a flipchart.

TRAINER'S NOTES

It's not uncommon for questions put in the Parking Lot to be answered later as part of the training. It may be that the trainer simply wants to leave that item or topic until later in the session.

Flies Away

ITCMXL

TIME REQUIRED	SIZE OF GROUP	MATERIAL REQUIRED
5 minutes.	Unlimited, but need to be broken into groups of 5 to 7 people.	None.

Overview

A simple problem to get the group thinking.

Goal

To energise the group.

Procedure

1. Break the larger group into groups of 5 to 7 people.
2. Tell each team they have a simple problem to solve.
3. Here is the problem. If you had a sealed jar on a set of scales with 6 flies asleep inside it and you shook the jar to make the flies move, would the weight of the jar and the flies be more, less or the same once you had shaken the jar?
4. You could award a small prize to the first group to give the correct answer and explanation of their solution.

Discussion points

1. How does this type of process relate to what we are doing here?
2. How does this relate to our workplace?

Variations

None.

Solution

The weight of the jar and the flies doesn't change. In order to fly, the flies must produce downward air currents that are equal in force to their weight. Therefore, whether standing or in flight, the insects push down with the same force.

TRAINER'S NOTES

36

Last Resort

TIME REQUIRED	SIZE OF GROUP	MATERIAL REQUIRED
30–40 minutes.	Unlimited.	Each team will require a sheet of flipchart paper and pens.

Overview

This is a team-building activity that may be used at any time during training.

Goal

To develop a team approach to problem solving.

Procedure

1. Advise the group that they are going to be given a task to complete. The large group may be broken into smaller teams if necessary, but if the large group is to work as one team after the training it may be worthwhile keeping them together.
2. Tell them that the CEO has just decided to diversify from the core business of the company and build a holiday resort in an attempt to finally make some money.
3. Advise each team that they have been given the job of designing the 'perfect' resort and deciding on the perfect location for it. The project is to be completed within 20 minutes.
4. At the end of the 20 minutes ask one person (from each team) to give a presentation of the final design.

Discussion points

1. How did the team arrive at a consensus in the time frame allocated?
2. How were any differences resolved?
3. Did any leaders emerge?
4. How does this exercise apply in the workplace?

Variation

Other items may be designed rather than a holiday resort.

TRAINER'S NOTES

If all the participants are from the same company they can be told that this is a directive from their current CEO in step 2 of the procedure. If the participants are from a number of different companies they should be told that they have all been employed in a new company and that this is a directive from their new CEO.

Meeting Proposals

TCFXLPES

TIME REQUIRED	SIZE OF GROUP	MATERIAL REQUIRED
45–60 minutes.	Up to 24 but need to be broken into groups of 5 to 7.	One copy of the 'Meeting Proposals' handout for each person and a pen.

Overview

Here is another activity that can be used to improve meeting techniques.

Goals

1. To identify ways of making meetings run more effectively.
2. To demonstrate a team approach to problem solving.
3. To identify a set of meeting rules.

Procedure

1. Ask the large group to break into smaller groups of 5 to 7 people.
2. Give each person a copy of the 'Meeting Proposal' handout.
3. Tell each team that they now have 30 minutes in which to make proposals to improve the effectiveness of meetings. The proposals should include a set of meeting rules. The teams are allowed to organise themselves in whatever way they see fit, for example splitting into sub-groups for part of the time, having a chairperson, etc.
4. At the end of the 30 minutes, each team should have formulated specific proposals by either consensus or majority vote. Ask each team to give a short presentation on their proposals.

Discussion points

1. How can you make sure you follow these rules after today?
2. Why aren't these things being done at present?

Variation

Have all the small groups reach a consensus on the 'Top 20' rules after they have each given their presentation. If time is available they can also prioritise this list.

TRAINER'S NOTES

Meeting Proposals

1. How could we make our meetings run more effectively?

2. What problems do we currently have with our meetings?

3. What makes our meetings counterproductive?

4. What rules could be devised to make our meetings run more effectively?

_____

_____

_____

_____

_____

_____

_____

_____

_____

_____

_____

38

Service Secrets

TIME REQUIRED	SIZE OF GROUP	MATERIAL REQUIRED
10–20 minutes.	Unlimited.	One copy of the 'Customer Service Secrets' handout for each person along with a pen. One prepared 'Customer Service Secrets' overhead. One small prize.

Overview

This exercise can be used for any training to do with customer service.

Goals

1. To identify the key components of good customer service principles.
2. To energise the group.

Procedure

1. Towards the end of any training session involving customer service techniques, give a copy of the 'Customer Service Secrets' handout to everyone. The handout should be kept face down until participants are asked to turn it over.
2. Tell the group that they are going to have a quick quiz. The quiz will be in the form of a puzzle.
3. Ask the group to turn their sheets over. They will see 6 statements with missing words. All of the missing words are contained in the puzzle—the words may be shown backwards, forwards, or diagonally.
4. Tell the participants that the first person to circle all the correct words and fill in the blank spaces will be awarded a prize.
5. Once the first person has shown you the correct answers, the 'Customer Service Secrets' overhead can be used as a summary.

Discussion points

None.

Variation

This exercise can be used very effectively in small groups. Just give each team one copy of the handout. The winning team is then given a prize.

TRAINER'S NOTES

Service Secrets

The puzzle shown below has all the missing words hidden inside it. The words may be shown horizontally, vertically or diagonally and may go in any direction. Your job is to find all of the missing words. You must circle them and write the missing word in the places shown in the statements. The first one has been completed for you. As soon as you have completed the task, stand up.

1. Always use the customer's NAME
2. Say _____ and _____ ___ when asking customers for _____.
3. Explain your _____ when you have to say __ to a customer's request.
4. Show your _____ in the customer's needs.
5. Show _____ for the customer's feelings.
6. Let the customer know what their _____ are.
7. _____! Even if you're on the phone.

```
D  A  Y  H  O  L  I  T  A  D  Y  O  W  K  I
S  L  K  E  N  V  T  S  E  R  E  T  N  I  O
O  C  I  C  O  H  R  K  A  L  P  L  R  Y  L
W  A  Y  U  I  A  F  U  J  U  L  R  A  P  R
I  L  Y  E  T  S  N  O  S  A  E  R  U  U  P
R  E  E  M  A  N  E  F  E  H  A  Y  K  E  T
C  J  H  U  M  A  K  U  L  I  S  G  A  B  S
L  R  K  C  R  S  R  O  Y  E  E  L  C  N  O
E  J  L  A  O  A  L  Y  M  Y  L  L  O  G  D
F  E  H  E  F  F  N  K  E  H  C  I  I  E  R
O  U  I  L  N  J  O  N  U  B  T  B  N  M  O
U  Q  S  A  I  K  C  A  K  P  M  H  E  G  S
W  E  G  Y  C  I  F  H  O  C  E  L  I  O  S
T  O  M  E  M  P  A  T  H  Y  T  U  F  N  V
E  R  Z  A  N  O  M  E  P  I  H  A  X  I  A
```

Service Secrets Solution

Customer Service Secrets

1. Always use the customer's NAME.

2. Say PLEASE and THANK YOU when asking customers for INFORMATION.

3. Explain your REASONS when you have to say NO to a customer's request.

4. Show your INTEREST in the customer's needs

5. Show EMPATHY for the customer's feelings.

6. Let the customer know what their OPTIONS are.

7. SMILE! Even if you're on the phone.

Ideas 'R' Us

ITMXL

TIME REQUIRED	SIZE OF GROUP	MATERIAL REQUIRED
20–30 minutes.	Up to 24 but need to be broken into groups of 5 to 7.	One copy of the 'Ideas 'R' Us' handout and a pen for each person.

Overview

An activity to promote creativity.

Goals

1. To get participants thinking creatively.
2. To energise the group.

Procedure

1. Break the large group into smaller groups of 5 to 7 people.
2. Let the groups know that a lot of successful companies are always looking for creative people. This is an opportunity for the participants to demonstrate how creative they are.
3. Give each participant a copy of the 'Ideas 'R' Us' handout and a pen. You can use the second, more challenging sheet if necessary, or just stick with the first handout.
4. Tell the group that they now have 10 to 15 minutes to come up with as many ideas as they can to help the following businesses promote their services. The ideas need to be creative and unique and offer something different from each company's competitors.
5. Stress that the ideas and suggestions should be consistent with what the business offers. For example, a sporting goods business shouldn't be offering packets of free Post-It Notes®. There are no budget constraints.
6. After the 15 minute period, ask each group to give a quick summary of their ideas. A vote may be taken as to which is the most creative idea, and a prize awarded.
7. You can now lead a discussion into the area of creativity and perhaps what some of the barriers to creativity are.

Discussion points

1. Why is it that a lot of people resist creative thinking?
2. How does this relate to our training session?
3. How does this relate to our workplace?

Variations

1. The exercise could be modified to suggest creative ways of promoting particular sports, cars, restaurants, etc.
2. On completion of this exercise (while the participants are still in a creative mood), it may be worthwhile getting them to look at creative ideas for their own business.

TRAINER'S NOTES

Ideas 'R' Us

Business name: Books 'R' Us
Type of business: Bookshop
Ideas/suggestions: _____
_____
_____
_____

Business name: Courses 'R' Us
Type of business: Adult training
Ideas/suggestions: _____
_____
_____
_____

Business name: Repairs 'R' Us
Type of business: Mechanical repairs
Ideas/suggestions: _____
_____
_____
_____

Business name: Dollars 'R' Us
Type of business: Financial services
Ideas/suggestions: _____
_____
_____
_____

Business name: Properties 'R' Us
Type of business: Property development
Ideas/suggestions: _____
_____
_____
_____

Business name: Flowers 'R' Us
Type of business: Nursery and garden supplies
Ideas/suggestions: _____
_____
_____
_____

Ideas 'R' Us

Business name: Adult Toys 'R' Us
Type of business: Adult novelty shop
Ideas/suggestions: _____

_____

_____

Business name: Funerals 'R' Us
Type of business: Funeral home
Ideas/suggestions: _____

_____

_____

Business name: Escorts 'R' Us
Type of business: Escort/dating service
Ideas/suggestions: _____

_____

_____

Business name: Spies 'R' Us
Type of business: Private investigations
Ideas/suggestions: _____

_____

_____

Business name: Divorces 'R' Us
Type of business: Solicitors specialising in divorces
Ideas/suggestions: _____

_____

_____

Business name: Guns 'R' Us
Type of business: Gun shop and supplies
Ideas/suggestions: _____

_____

_____

40

Doodleloo

IL

TIME REQUIRED	SIZE OF GROUP	MATERIAL REQUIRED
None.	Unlimited.	A paper tablecloth for each participant table and lots of coloured marking pens.

Overview

An activity to help people stay alert in a lengthy presentation.

Goals

1. To keep people focused during training.
2. To gain feedback.
3. To have some fun during a long or very dry training session.

Procedure

1. At the beginning of training point out that some people think better while doodling, while others find it easier to focus.
2. Tell the group that their tablecloths are made of paper and that the pens placed on the tables are to be used for doodling.
3. Encourage the participants to draw pictures and write down key words or questions that they think of.

4. During the training session, walk around to see how things are progressing and praise people who have taken advantage of the materials. You may also see questions that have been written and can be addressed as the training progresses.

Discussion points

None.

Variations

1. For training of longer duration, stick the tablecloths up for display. The table with the best or most creative (and relevant) set of doodles can be awarded a small prize.
2. Have the participants from different tables compare the results of this exercise before each break for a bit of fun.

TRAINER'S NOTES

All Scrambled Up

IMX

TIME REQUIRED	SIZE OF GROUP	MATERIAL REQUIRED
10–15 minutes during training. There is no time requirement if the activity is used before training starts.	Unlimited.	Each participant will require a copy of the 'All Scrambled Up' handout and a pen.

Overview

This activity can be used as a filler while waiting for people to come back from breaks, or at the start of training to keep people occupied while latecomers arrive.

Goals

1. To keep the early arrivals occupied.
2. To form initial teams within the group.
3. To fill in some time if required.

Procedure

1. As people start to arrive at the training session put them into groups of 3 and give them a copy of the 'All Scrambled Up' handout and a pen.
2. Tell the groups that you have an exercise for them to complete.
3. As each trio solves the puzzle, reward them. This is not only a reward for solving the puzzle, but also for arriving early enough to work on it. This should encourage participants to come back on time after breaks.

Discussion points

None.

Variation

Handouts can be placed on the tables with a set of written instructions. This could be conducted as a table exercise.

TRAINER'S NOTES

At the beginning of training, make sure everyone has put their handout away.

All Scrambled Up

Listed below are a number of words and names in different categories. The problem is that the letters have been scrambled. Your task is to work out what the words are.

Offices	Vehicles	Household	Animals	Food	Places
skupterdecom	rufudstaro	shobittelur	bitbar	blaavak	latadinh
nigrarseo	klirfoft	grinnafyp	odgin	kolochcateace	gremoxbulu
aleevemilopann	meatsirlier	ckallolcw	helptean	dreecifir	slipringaces
helpnouch	colormetcy	newchiminaghas	chinroores	stewbitsicuse	bruenmole
plastre	shipkebu	garfrerotier	chinead	whidescans	stagfanhian
dribngrein	cromeadraru	swhadshier	ogarokan	plepiaep	cromooc
laccurlato	wongvlakse	depleyavrio	frefiga	totorebe	fathrisouca

_____ _____ _____ _____ _____ _____

_____ _____ _____ _____ _____ _____

_____ _____ _____ _____ _____ _____

_____ _____ _____ _____ _____ _____

_____ _____ _____ _____ _____ _____

_____ _____ _____ _____ _____ _____

_____ _____ _____ _____ _____ _____

All Scrambled Up Solution

Offices	Vehicles	Household	Animals	Food	Places
computer desk	ford taurus	toilet brush	rabbit	baklava	Thailand
organiser	forklift	frying pan	dingo	chocolate cake	Luxembourg
manila envelope	semitrailer	wall clock	elephant	fried rice	Alice Springs
hole punch	motorcycle	washing machine	rhinoceros	sweet biscuits	Melbourne
stapler	pushbike	refrigerator	echidna	sandwiches	Afghanistan
ring binder	armoured car	dishwasher	kangaroo	apple pie	Morocco
calculator	volkswagen	video player	giraffe	beetroot	South Africa

42

Balloon Races

TIME REQUIRED	SIZE OF GROUP	MATERIAL REQUIRED
5 minutes.	Unlimited.	One balloon for each pair of participants (plus a few spares). A roll of masking tape will also be required.

Overview

This is a lively activity to get the blood flowing.

Goals

1. To energise the group.
2. To demonstrate cooperative power.
3. To have some fun.

Procedure

1. Ask everyone in the group to select a partner.
2. After they have done this, give each pair a balloon and tell them to inflate it and tie it off.
3. While this is being done stick 2 lengths of masking tape on the floor about 10 metres apart (the further the better). The tape should go right across the room. One marker will indicate the start and finish line, the other the point the teams must run to.
4. After all the balloons have been inflated and tied off, ask the participants to come back behind the 'starting line'.

5. Advise the teams that they will be having a relay race. To win the race they must be the first pair to get to the other line and back again with their balloon.
6. Explain that the only rules are that the balloon must be intact when the team finishes, they are not allowed to use their hands or arms to hold the balloon during the race, the balloon must be carried by both members of the team during the race (i.e. not between one person's legs), and they must not allow the balloon to touch the floor. If any of these rules are broken the team is to come back to the starting line and begin again.
7. After the race has been completed and the winner identified a prize should be awarded.

Discussion points

None.

Variations

1. Can be done in trios.
2. Can be done outdoors.

TRAINER'S NOTES

Add 'em Up

IMX

TIME REQUIRED	SIZE OF GROUP	MATERIAL REQUIRED
2 minutes.	Unlimited.	One prepared 'Add 'em Up' overhead.

Overview

A quick activity that can be used at any time during training.

Goals

1. To fill in time while people come back from breaks.
2. To develop a sense of competition.

Procedure

1. Display the 'Add 'em Up' overhead while waiting for the last few participants to return from a break.
2. Tell the group that they need to work out what the missing numbers are. The correct numbers will make all of the rows, columns and diagonals add up to the same number.
3. The first person to get the answer can be given a prize.

Discussion points

None.

Variation

Can be done as a very quick small group exercise.

Solution

8	1	**6**
3	5	**7**
1	9	**2**

TRAINER'S NOTES

Add 'em up

8	1	?
3	5	?
1	9	?

Missing Matches

IMX

TIME REQUIRED	SIZE OF GROUP	MATERIAL REQUIRED
2 minutes.	Unlimited.	One prepared 'Missing Matches' overhead.

Overview

Another quick activity that can be used at any time during training.

Goals

1. To fill in time while people come back from breaks.
2. To develop a sense of competition.

Procedure

1. While waiting for the last few participants to return from a break, display the 'Missing Matches' overhead.
2. Tell the group that they have to take 4 matches away from the pattern to leave 4 complete triangles.
3. The first person to give the correct answer should win a prize.

Discussion points

None.

Variation

Can be done as a very quick small group exercise.

Solution

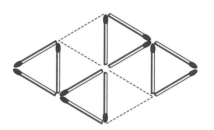

TRAINER'S NOTES

Missing Matches

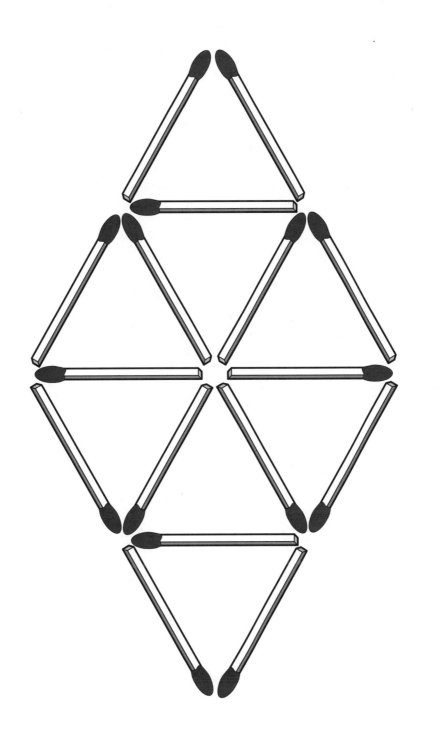

45

Missing Numbers

IMX

TIME REQUIRED	SIZE OF GROUP	MATERIAL REQUIRED
2 minutes.	Unlimited.	A prepared 'Missing Numbers' overhead.

Overview

Another quick activity that can be used at any time during training.

Goals

1. To fill in time while people come back from breaks.
2. To develop a sense of competition.

Procedure

1. Display the 'Missing Numbers' overhead while waiting for the last few participants to return from a break.
2. Tell the group that they have to work out what the next 2 numbers are in the sequence and why.
3. The first person to give the correct answer wins a prize.

Discussion points

None.

Variations

1. Can be done as a very quick small group exercise.
2. A whiteboard may be used in place of the overhead.

Solution

The next 2 numbers are 7 and 6. The pattern is formed by spelling out the numbers and arranging the words in alphabetical order.

8 Eight
5 Five
4 Four
9 Nine
1 One
7 Seven
6 Six

TRAINER'S NOTES

Missing Numbers

8 5 4 9 1 ? ? ?

Centre of Operations

ITCFMXLPS

TIME REQUIRED	SIZE OF GROUP	MATERIAL REQUIRED
20–30 minutes.	Unlimited, but a large group will need to be broken into smaller groups of 5 to 7 people.	Each team will require a sheet of flipchart paper and pens.

Overview

This is a team-building activity that can be used at any time during training.

Goals

1. To develop a team approach to problem solving.
2. To encourage participants to think of ways of improving their office layout.
3. To improve time-management skills.

Procedure

1. Break the large group into smaller groups of 5 to 7 people.
2. Advise the group that they are going to be given a task to complete.
3. Tell them that their task is to design the 'perfect' office layout. The task is to be completed in 10 minutes.
4. An unlimited budget has been set aside for this purpose but the team must demonstrate that any expenditure will improve productivity. Too many people have been complaining about cramped offices and how this is affecting time usage.

5. After the designs have been completed, have one person (from each team) give a presentation of their final office design.
6. A vote may be carried out at the end of the team presentations to see who has the best design. A small prize may be awarded to the winning team.

Discussion points

1. How did the team arrive at a consensus within the time frame allocated?
2. How were any differences resolved?
3. What time-management problems were identified?
4. How can these ideas be applied in the workplace?

Variation

Advise the group that they may move things in their existing offices, but are not allowed to purchase anything new. They are also allowed to 'borrow' any spare equipment that they know is not currently being used.

TRAINER'S NOTES

47

New Talent

ITM

TIME REQUIRED	SIZE OF GROUP	MATERIAL REQUIRED
As long as required. The briefing only takes a minute during the training, and the 'show' is usually presented during an evening dinner.	The bigger the better.	None.

Overview

This activity is for use on courses of a longer duration and with larger sized groups. It is usually conducted as an evening activity.

Goal

To develop a sense of team spirit.

Procedure

1. Advise the group that they will be having a dinner one evening of the training program and that during or after the dinner there will be a talent quest.
2. Tell the group that volunteers will be needed to participate in the quest either as solo acts or in groups.
3. Anyone wanting to take part in the talent quest should advise you beforehand.
4. After the talent quest, the audience should vote for the best performance. The winner, along with all the other acts, should be given a prize.

Discussion points

None.

Variation

Groups may be formed and given the briefing that they are each to do a 2-minute act.

TRAINER'S NOTES

A to Z

ITCMXS

TIME REQUIRED	SIZE OF GROUP	MATERIAL REQUIRED
5–10 minutes.	Unlimited.	A prepared 'A to Z' overhead.

Overview

A quick activity that can be used at any time during training.

Goals

1. To fill in time while people come back from breaks.
2. To develop a sense of competition.

Procedure

1. While waiting for the last few participants to return from a break, display the 'A to Z' overhead.
2. Tell the group that they need to use each of the 26 letters of the alphabet (only once) to complete the words shown on the overhead.
3. The first person to tell you the missing letters should be given a prize.

Discussion points (if used as a team exercise)

1. What was the problem? How was it broken down? Who did what?

2. Did any leaders emerge?
3. What time-management issues were identified?
4. How does this relate to what we do at work?

Variations

1. Can be done as a very quick small group exercise.
2. A handout may be used in place of the overhead.

Solution

1. Plastered
2. Jaws
3. Frozen
4. Gnome
5. Shave
6. Blocking
7. Quote
8. Sixty

TRAINER'S NOTES

A to Z

1. _ A _ _ E E _ _

2. _ A _ S _

3. _ _ R O _ N

4. _ _ O _ E

5. S _ _ _ E

6. _ L O _ _ ING

7. _ _ _ _ TE

8. S _ _ T _

49

Who's Important?

ITMP

TIME REQUIRED	SIZE OF GROUP	MATERIAL REQUIRED
15–20 minutes.	Up to 24, but large groups will need to be broken into smaller groups of 3 or 4 people.	Each participant should get a copy of the 'Who's Important?' handout. A sheet of flipchart paper and marking pens will also be required for each group.

Overview

An easy activity to get participants talking to each other.

Goals

1. To encourage conversation.
2. To help the participants find out a little about each other.

Procedure

1. Break the large group into smaller groups of 3 or 4 people.
2. Give each person a copy of the 'Who's Important?' handout.
3. Tell each group that they have 10 minutes to identify the 10 most important people since 1952 and then rank them in priority order.

4. After the task has been completed, ask a volunteer from each group to state who the group has selected, and why.

Discussion points

1. Why did the groups select who they did?
2. Who selected the most unusual person?
3. What did the participants find out about their fellow team members?

Variation

You could narrow this down to a specific profession; for example, sports people, musicians, politicians, actors, etc.

TRAINER'S NOTES

Who's Important?

Your group will have 10 minutes to identify (and rank in priority order) who you consider to be the 10 most important people since 1952.

1.

2.

3.

4.

5.

6.

7.

8.

9.

10.

Sacked or Promoted?

IMXLPS

TIME REQUIRED	SIZE OF GROUP	MATERIAL REQUIRED
2–10 minutes.	Unlimited.	Each participant will require a pen and paper.

Overview

This activity can be used in many applications, from an icebreaker to an introduction to change management.

Goals

1. To make participants experience a simple change exercise.
2. To make participants perform a task under pressure.

Procedure

1. Start this activity by telling the group that the CEO of the company is going to implement a number of changes within the organisation. These changes have been determined by the Board of Directors and are not open to discussion.
2. Also tell the participants that any employee who cannot perform their tasks in the new way may be fired.
3. Inform the group that the first change is being implemented immediately and that, as of now, all employees will be required to do all their written correspondence using only their left hand.
4. To test this new system, all staff members must be able to write the letters of the alphabet legibly with their left hand in less than 30 seconds.
5. Advise the group that any staff members unable to carry out the task in less than 30 seconds will be terminated. If the task is completed in the time period but is illegible the staff member will be terminated. Any staff members who complete the activity correctly will be considered for promotion.
6. At the end of the 30 seconds go around the room, check everyone's results and indicate whether they are now unemployed or eligible for promotion.

Discussion points

1. How did everyone feel about this exercise?
2. How do people feel about forced change?
3. How do people perform under stress?
4. Why did some people find this exercise easier than others?
5. How did the left-handed people feel about the test?
6. What did the right-handed people think of the left-handed people and the advantage they had?
7. How does this relate to our workplace?

Variation

The attached briefing sheet may be used instead of the verbal briefing.

Source

Adapted from a game suggested by Nathan Rothchild, New South Wales.

TRAINER'S NOTES

The first part of this exercise should be presented 'seriously' by the trainer.

Memo

From: Managing Director
To: all employees
Subject: change

As you are all aware, we are going through a period of change. We need to ensure that all our staff are totally flexible and can adapt quickly to change.

The Board of Directors met late last night to discuss this issue. It was decided that we only want to retain employees that can adapt quickly to change in the workplace.

Therefore, as of this moment, all employees must do all their written correspondence using only their left hand.

Obviously, as with any new task, we must have some means of evaluating the performance of this new requirement. Every employee will be required to write the letters of the alphabet using their left hand, in a time frame of 30 seconds. At the end of the 30 second period all 26 letters must be written correctly and legibly. Any person failing to do this will be immediately terminated. Staff who complete this exercise correctly will be retained and considered for promotion.

Your facilitator will have you carry out the exercise and will evaluate your results.

Good luck.

Repeat After Me

TIME REQUIRED	SIZE OF GROUP	MATERIAL REQUIRED
30–60 minutes.	Unlimited, but larger groups will need to be broken into smaller groups of 5 to 7 participants.	One copy of the 'Repeat After Me' handout and a pen for each participant.

Overview

An activity that allows participants to identify ways of improving their communication or customer service skills.

Goals

1. To identify ways of overcoming communication barriers.
2. To improve listening skills.

Procedure

1. Start this exercise by breaking the large group into smaller groups of 5 to 7 people.
2. Advise the groups that they are going to be involved in an exercise to look at ways of overcoming communication barriers.
3. Give each person a copy of the 'Repeat After Me' handout and a pen and allow them 15 minutes to look for solutions to each of the questions shown on the handout.
4. At the end of the 15 minutes have each group give feedback on their suggestions.

Discussion points

1. Which group had the best ideas?
2. Why don't we do these things automatically?
3. What are the 10 best ideas? Can these be a set of rules for us to use?

Variation

Handouts can be given to the participants to fill in individually before forming groups.

TRAINER'S NOTES

Repeat After Me

1. What would you do if you were trying to talk with someone in a noisy workplace? How could you make it easier to communicate?

2. What would you do if you were trying to talk with someone and there were lots of visual distractions around? How could you make it easier to communicate?

3. What would you do if you were trying to talk with someone and you felt really tired? How could you make it easier to communicate?

4. What would you do if you were trying to talk with someone and they had a very strong accent? How could you make it easier to communicate?

5. What would you do if you were trying to talk with someone and they were speaking too fast for you to understand? How could you make it easier to communicate?

6. What would you do if you were trying to talk with someone and they were speaking too slowly or softly? How could you make it easier to communicate?

7. What would you do if you were trying to talk with someone and they kept using jargon words or terms you didn't understand? How could you make it easier to communicate?

8. What would you do if you were trying to talk with someone and they appeared to be very stressed? How could you make it easier to communicate?

9. What would you do if you were trying to talk with someone and they were using emotionally charged words or statements? How could you make it easier to communicate?

10. What would you do if you were trying to talk with someone and they were verbally attacking you? How could you make it easier to communicate?

52

Name That Tune

TIME REQUIRED	SIZE OF GROUP	MATERIAL REQUIRED
5 minutes.	Unlimited, but a large group needs to be broken into smaller groups of 5 to 7 people.	A cassette player and a prepared audio tape with lots of theme songs (or music) from television shows, both old and new.

Overview

Here is an activity that can be used to get people back on time after a break.

Goal

To get people back into the room on time after a break.

Procedure

1. Before having a break, advise the group that there will be a fun competition when the group is due to start again.
2. Break the large group into teams of 3 to 4 people.
3. Tell the group that they must be back in the room to participate. All team members must be in the room for the team to play. Also let them know that prizes will be awarded.
4. When it's time to recommence, let the group know that you will be playing a number of theme songs or music from television shows.
5. The first team to identify each song will get a point.
6. The team with the most points wins a prize.

Discussion points

None.

Variation

You may want to play the first theme before going to the break as a sample of what is to come.

TRAINER'S NOTES

Pyramid Puzzle

IMX

TIME REQUIRED	SIZE OF GROUP	MATERIAL REQUIRED
2 minutes.	Unlimited.	One prepared 'Pyramid Puzzle' overhead.

Overview

Another quick activity that can be used at any time during training to promote competition.

Goals

1. To fill in time while people come back from breaks.
2. To develop a sense of competition.

Procedure

1. While waiting for the last few participants to return from a break, display the 'Pyramid Puzzle' overhead.
2. Tell the group that there is a word hidden in each line of the pyramid. Each symbol represents a letter. Their task is to tell you what the 5 words are.
3. The first person to give you the correct answer should be given a prize.

Discussion points

None.

Variations

1. This can used effectively as a small group exercise.
2. A whiteboard could be used in place of the overhead.

Solution

= A, = S, = W, = P.

A
AS
WAS
WASP
WASPS

TRAINER'S NOTES

Pyramid Puzzle

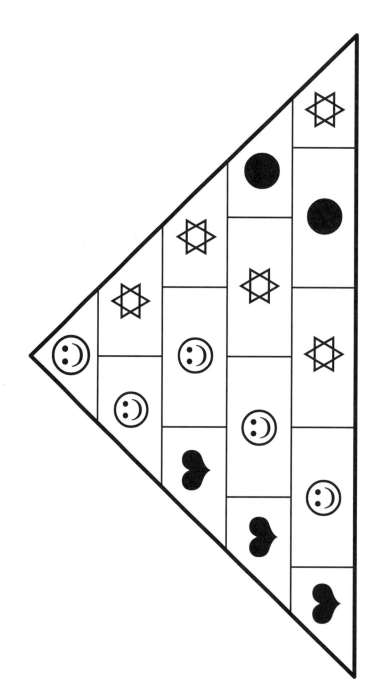

54

External Limitations

TIME REQUIRED	SIZE OF GROUP	MATERIAL REQUIRED
5–10 minutes.	Unlimited.	One large cardboard box (sealed) with something inside it (not too heavy).

Overview

This activity demonstrates how people perform when limitations are put on them. It can also be used to promote awareness in relation to people with disabilities and to encourage safe lifting techniques.

Goals

1. To demonstrate how difficult it can be to perform a task when various constraints are imposed.
2. To show how people can adapt to overcome imposed constraints.

Procedure

1. Start this exercise by asking for a volunteer from the group.
2. When the volunteer is at the front of the room, ask them to pick the cardboard box up (demonstrating safe lifting techniques) and place it on the table.
3. Now ask them to place the box back on the floor.
4. Next ask them to place one hand behind their back and repeat the procedure.
5. If this task is accomplished, ask them to put the box back on the floor again.

6. Now ask them to put one hand behind their back and lift one foot off the floor and repeat the exercise.
7. A discussion can be led into the various constraints we have placed on us in the workplace and how they might limit our ability to perform certain tasks.

Discussion points

1. How did our volunteer feel during the activity?
2. What constraints are placed on us in the workplace that interfere with our performance?
3. How can we overcome constraints that are imposed on us?

Variation

This activity can be taken further and used as a problem-solving exercise (i.e. how can we perform this task effectively and safely even with particular constraints placed on us?).

Source

Adapted from a game suggested by Jeff Donnelly, New South Wales.

TRAINER'S NOTES

Ensure that safe lifting practices are adhered to at all times and that there is no possibility of your volunteer/s hurting themselves.

55

Good Sports

TIME REQUIRED	SIZE OF GROUP	MATERIAL REQUIRED
5 minutes.	Up to 40.	One 'Good Sports' cutout for each participant.

Overview

Here is a lively activity to help the participants break into small groups (with some fun thrown in).

Goals

1. To break a large group into smaller random groups.
2. To energise the participants.
3. To have some fun.

Procedure

1. If a large group needs to be broken into smaller groups this activity will help. Begin by randomly handing out one 'Good Sports' cutout to each participant. Advise them not to let anyone see what they have.
2. Explain to the group that every person has a 'Good Sports' cutout and they are now to find people with matching sports cutouts. The catch is that they are not allowed to show their card to anyone else, and they are not allowed to speak. Therefore, each participant will have to demonstrate their sport so others can see what they have. This is a nonverbal exercise.

3. When the groups have formed, the training can move on in the relevant area.

Discussion points

None.

Variations

Make other cards showing different professions.

TRAINER'S NOTES

Good Sports

56

What Did You See?

IFMXPS

TIME REQUIRED	SIZE OF GROUP	MATERIAL REQUIRED
5–10 minutes.	Unlimited.	One copy of the 'What Did You See?' handout for each participant and a pen.

Overview

This quick icebreaker can be used to allow participants to introduce themselves to someone else in the group and to demonstrate how observant, or unobservant, some people are.

Goal

To demonstrate how observant, or unobservant, some people are.

Procedure

1. Start by asking all the participants to stand and form pairs.
2. After the pairs have been formed, ask the individuals in each pair to face each other and introduce themselves for about 30 seconds.
3. When the introductions have finished, ask each partner to turn their back on the other person so that they are out of sight.
4. Hand everyone a copy of the 'What Did You See?' handout and a pen.
5. Tell them that they have about 1 minute to fill in the requested details.

6. After they have completed the questionnaire, ask them to turn around and see how many answers they got right.
7. Ask for a show of hands from people who got all 10 questions correct. If no hands go up, ask for 9 correct answers and work down from there.
8. The person/s with the highest score should be acknowledged and perhaps awarded a small prize.

Discussion points

1. Who had the highest score?
2. Why is it that some people seem to be more observant than others?
3. How can we improve our powers of observation?

Variation

Can be conducted as a small group activity where teams are formed and the individuals introduce themselves to each other. After the introductions have been carried out, have the groups move out of sight of each other. Give each person in the group copies of the 'What Did You See?' handout to complete.

TRAINER'S NOTES

What Did You See?

There is an old saying that goes, 'I can remember the face, but not the name'. Perhaps we aren't as observant as we think we are!

You have just spent some time talking with your partner and introducing yourselves to each other, so you should know the other person reasonably well. Let's test this assumption.

Listed below are 10 questions. Please read through them and answer them as you go. Don't try to guess the answer, only write it down if you are absolutely sure.

1. What is your partner's first name?

_____

2. What is their surname?

_____

3. What is the colour of their eyes?

_____

4. Are they wearing glasses? If so, please describe them.

_____

5. What is the colour of their hair?

_____

6. How tall are they (approximately)?

_____

7. What types of jewellery do they have on?

_____

8. How are they dressed?

_____

9. What colour shoes do they have on?

_____

10. What other distinguishing features do they have?

_____

Total correct [   ]

57

Can't Lose!

TCMX

TIME REQUIRED	SIZE OF GROUP	MATERIAL REQUIRED
10–20 minutes.	Unlimited, but a large group will need to be broken into smaller groups of 3 or 4 people.	Each team will require a copy of the 'Can't Lose!' handout and a pen.

Overview

Here is an interesting problem-solving activity that may be used at any time during training.

Goals

1. To demonstrate the benefit of synergy.
2. To improve teamwork.

Procedure

1. Break the large group into smaller teams of 3 or 4 people.
2. Give each team a copy of the 'Can't Lose!' handout.
3. Tell the groups that they are to solve the problem given to them. The team with the first set of correct answers will be given a prize.

Discussion points

1. Which team got the correct answers?
2. How were the answers achieved?
3. What helped the team solve this problem?
4. What problems did each team encounter?
5. How does this relate to the workplace?

Variations

1. A time limit may be set.
2. Can be done individually if required.

Solution

First name	Beverly	Eddie	Jo	Nick
Surname	Wecski	Hunter	Slaviki	Chang
Amount bet	$400	$870	$550	$640
Got back	$520	$760	$450	$560

TRAINER'S NOTES

Can't Lose!

Four friends (Beverly, Eddie, Jo and Nick) decided to go to the races one day. They were each equipped with an infallible betting system for picking race winners. To gain entry to the races they had to pre-book their entry tickets. The tickets were booked under their surnames (Chang, Hunter, Slaviki and Wecski). At the end of the day they discussed their results. The totals bet by each person were: $400, $550, $640 and $870. The amount each person collected was: $450, $520, $560 and $760. As a team, you need to identify each person's full name, the sum of money bet by each person, and how much each person got back. All the information you need to work this out is shown below.

Clues:

1. Beverly Wecski made a modest profit, getting back $120 more than she bet.
2. Slaviki got back $450. Her outlay was not $640.
3. Jo paid out $550.
4. Eddie's surname isn't Chang.
5. Nick wasn't the person who bet $870 to get back $760.

First name			
Surname			
Amount bet			
Amount collected			

58

XO Test

XLE

TIME REQUIRED	SIZE OF GROUP	MATERIAL REQUIRED
10–15 minutes.	6 to 24 people.	Whiteboard and marking pen, plus a set of prepared questions (need to be challenging).

Overview

This activity can be used at the end of training to test the participants' knowledge.

Goal

To check the participants' knowledge at the end of training.

Procedure

1. At the end of training let the group know that they are going to be tested on the knowledge they have gained. The text will be in the form of a quiz with a winning team identified.
2. Split the group into two teams. One team will be the Xs and the other the Os.
3. A large tick-tack-toe game grid should be drawn on the whiteboard.
4. Advise the groups that you will be asking a series of questions based on the concepts learnt in training. Each team will be asked a question. If they answer it correctly, they can put their X or O on the board. If they can't answer the question they are unable to take their move and the other team has a chance at answering it. If however the other team does get the correct answer they are not able to make a move as moves can only be made by the first team asked the question.
5. Flip a coin to see which team is asked the first question.
6. The team to get 3 Xs or Os in a row wins.

Discussion points

None.

Variations

1. Instead of using a whiteboard, a prepared overhead transparency could be used.
2. A large tick-tack-toe grid can be made on the floor using masking tape (about 3 metres square). As teams correctly answer the questions, the person answering the question can move into a square. Once someone is placed in a square they must remain silent.

TRAINER'S NOTES

XO Test

59

Time-management Quiz

TIME REQUIRED	SIZE OF GROUP	MATERIAL REQUIRED
5 minutes.	Unlimited.	Each participant will require a copy of the 'Time-management Quiz' handout and a pen.

Overview

Here is a good opening exercise for a time-management course.

Goal

To see how good people currently are with their time-management skills.

Procedure

1. During the start of the course give all the participants a copy of the 'Time-management Quiz'.

2. Ask the participants to look at the handout. They will see 10 questions and a ranking scale above them. They are to read through each question and score themselves using the scale. After all the scores have been written down they need to be totalled at the bottom of the page.

3. Depending on how honest the participants have been with their answers, this is what the scores indicate. This can be used as a script if necessary.

   0–9 Well done. People who score between 0 and 9 finish work on Friday afternoon, go home, and enjoy their weekend, because they know there is nothing outstanding or overlooked.

   10–25 Not too bad. People who score in this range know there is room for improvement. They finish work on Friday afternoon and go home to enjoy their weekend, but all of a sudden, sometime during Saturday, remember there's still a couple of outstanding jobs that need to be done.

   26–50 Congratulations! Congratulations on turning up today! This kind of person finishes work on a Friday afternoon and goes home, but they don't enjoy themselves at all. They spend their whole weekend worrying about the 27 projects still sitting on their desk, because they know that there will be other things coming in next week that will bury the projects already sitting there.

4. After explaining the scores (and waiting for the laughter to subside) move into a discussion on helping participants improve their time-management skills.

Discussion points

None.

Variation

If the group members know each other well they can be paired up and asked to fill in each other's quiz. That will add a touch of objectivity, if necessary.

Source for time-management tips

Kroehnert, Gary, **Taming Time: How Do You Eat An Elephant?**, McGraw-Hill Australia, Sydney, 1999.

TRAINER'S NOTES

Time-management Quiz

Read the 10 statements below and select the number from the scale that most closely matches your response to each statement. Write the number in the space provided to the left of each question. When all statements have been completed total the 10 numbers.

0	1	2	3	4	5
Never	Very infrequently	Sometimes	Frequently	Mostly	Always

1. _____ I think I'm indispensable. I often find myself taking on various jobs because I think I'm the only one who can do them.

2. _____ I don't have time to do all the important things because I'm too busy with smaller things that always pop up during the day.

3. _____ I tend to attempt to do too much. I usually say 'yes' to most requests as I feel I can do them all, or I don't want to upset people by saying 'no'.

4. _____ I feel continual pressure. I always seem to be behind and have no way of catching up. I feel as though I am always rushing.

5. _____ I work long hours: ten, eleven, twelve, sometimes up to fourteen hours a day, five or six days a week.

6. _____ I usually feel guilty about leaving work on time.

7. _____ I don't have enough time for rest, social activities or personal relationships.

8. _____ I constantly miss deadlines that have been set.

9. _____ I quite often take worries and problems home.

10. _____ I sometimes find it hard to make decisions and keep putting things off.

Your total score:

Mary's Lamb

ITCMS

TIME REQUIRED	SIZE OF GROUP	MATERIAL REQUIRED
5 minutes.	6 to 24 people.	One cut-out word for each participant. With small groups participants will get more than one.

Overview

This quick activity can be used to help participants improve their concentration.

Goals

1. To improve participants' concentration.
2. To energise the group.

Procedure

1. Start this activity by having all the participants form a circle. The circle can be made with or without chairs.
2. Once the circle has been formed, give each participant a cut-out word from the following page. If there are fewer than 16 participants, some people will get more than one word; if there are more than 16 people more than one set of cutouts will be needed. The cutouts are numbered and should be handed out in the correct sequence.
3. When everyone has their piece of paper, ask the first person (cutout number 1) to say their word.

Ask the next person to follow and so on until the group understands what needs to be done.
4. The result is usually a collection of disconnected words uttered at random. Tell the group to keep rehearsing until they have free-flowing sentences.

Discussion points

None.

Variations

1. The cutouts could be handed out at random. This would initiate a problem-solving activity to start with because participants would have to find out what the message is initially (the numbers will have to be removed from the cutouts for this). You could then move on to the exercise, but with participants still in their original positions (i.e. out of order).
2. Other prose can be used such as a very short story, a nursery rhyme, or perhaps you could write your own.

TRAINER'S NOTES

Mary's Lamb

1. Mary	2. had	3. a	4. little
5. lamb	6. and	7. everywhere	8. that
9. Mary	10. went	11. the	12. lamb
13. was	14. sure	15. to	16. go

Up or Down?

IMX

TIME REQUIRED	SIZE OF GROUP	MATERIAL REQUIRED
2 minutes.	Unlimited.	One prepared 'Up or Down?' overhead.

Overview

Another quick activity that can be used at any time during training. It is especially useful after breaks.

Goals

1. To fill in time while people come back from breaks.
2. To develop a sense of competition.

Procedure

1. Display the 'Up or Down?' overhead while waiting for the last few participants to return from a break.
2. Ask the group to explain why some letters are shown above the line (up) and some are shown below the line (down). In other words, what do the different sets of letters have in common?
3. Tell the group that the first person to give you the correct answer will win a prize.

Discussion points

None.

Variations

1. Can be done as a very quick small group exercise.
2. A whiteboard may be used in place of the overhead.

Solution

The letters on the top row consist of straight lines only, while the letters on the bottom row include curves.

TRAINER'S NOTES

Up or Down?

A B C D E F G H I

62

Doug's Dog

IMXP

TIME REQUIRED	SIZE OF GROUP	MATERIAL REQUIRED
2–5 minutes.	Unlimited.	None.

Overview

Here is a quick exercise that may be used while waiting for the last few participants to return from a break. It may also be used at the beginning of any training activities of a mathematical nature.

Goals

1. To keep participants occupied while waiting for stragglers to come back after a break.
2. To warm the group up when introducing training involving maths.

Procedure

1. During the beginning of training read out the following story. Doug had a cute little dog called Dasher which he liked very much. Unfortunately for Doug his girlfriend, Donna, also liked Dasher. Donna liked her so much that she offered to buy Dasher from Doug. So Donna offered Doug $20 for Dasher, which was all she could really afford. Doug reluctantly sold Dasher to Donna. However, Doug missed Dasher so much that he gave Donna $40 the next day and took Dasher back home. Donna still wanted Dasher, so she saved up another $20 and offered Doug $60. Poor Doug didn't like to refuse, so he gave Donna Dasher and took the $60. That night, Doug felt fed up with the whole business, so he went back to Donna and gave her $80 and took Dasher back.

2. Ask the group if anyone made a profit from these transactions and, if so, who did and how much (the story may have to be read a second time). Answers should be written down and not shown to anyone.

3. After an appropriate amount of time, ask each participant their answers—this will show how people perceived the information differently.

Discussion points

1. Why did some people have different answers?
2. If used as a small group exercise (see Variation section), ask how many people would have been able to answer the question by themselves?
3. How does this relate to the training we are about to begin?

Variation

The story can be read (once) for all the participants to listen to, then the briefing can be given. Rather than have each individual formulate an answer, form sub-groups of 3 or 4 people and get the group to give an answer. This will also demonstrate the benefit of synergy.

Solution

Donna made a profit of $40 and Doug lost $40.

TRAINER'S NOTES

Aliens

ITCMXLS

TIME REQUIRED	SIZE OF GROUP	MATERIAL REQUIRED
1–1½ hours.	8 to 40 people, but the large group will need to be broken into smaller groups of 4 to 10 people.	One large key. One large training room with furniture. One roll of masking tape. One 'Aliens' briefing sheet for each group. Each participant will also require a pen and paper.

Overview

This activity can be used as an icebreaker on longer courses or as a stand-alone team-building activity.

Goals

1. To develop a sense of teamwork and team spirit.
2. To increase leadership awareness.
3. To energise the group.

Procedure

1. Before the exercise commences, you will need to place tape on the floor indicating the prison cells (each about 3 metres square). The cells should all be at one end of the room.
2. Introduce this activity by asking the large group to form smaller teams of 4 to 10 people.
3. Once the teams have been formed, they should be placed in the separate taped squares on the floor and given a copy of the 'Aliens' briefing sheet. Read through the sheet with them and answer any questions they may have.
4. Give the groups 5 minutes to design their new language, select who their ER will be, and load their memory bank.
5. At the end of 5 minutes send all the robots out of the room with their list of commands.
6. As soon as the ERs leave the room, rearrange the furniture; for example, move some tables and explain to the groups that this is now a tunnel that the ERs must go through to get the key.
7. Tell the groups that the aliens are also moving the key to a different location. The key should be placed in a different location, perhaps somewhere where the ERs will not be able to see it.
8. Now go out to the ERs and brief them. They are only to follow the directions given to them by their group and not improvise at all. Remind them they are all very basic model ERs and have no problem-solving chips installed. Tell them that the aliens are relocating them to different cells but because they are robots that shouldn't make any difference to them. Take all the lists of commands from the ERs and redistribute them, ensuring no one gets the same sheet back. The robots should also be told that if they happen to bump into another robot, or any other obstacle, they will go into freeze mode and remain absolutely still until the next command is given that they can follow.
9. Bring the ERs back into the room and stand them in a line at the side of the room.
10. Advise the ETTs of the reassignment of the robots.
11. Remain silent—someone will realise what is happening and start calling out instructions.
12. Sit back and watch the fun, and confusion!
13. After the exercise, lead into a discussion on teamwork, multicultural issues, communication, etc. This activity covers a range of topics.

Discussion points

1. How do the ERs feel? How did they feel during the activity?
2. How do the ETTs feel? How did they feel during the activity?

Variations

1. This activity may be conducted outdoors.
2. Do not give out briefing sheets, just read the briefing to the groups.

TRAINER'S NOTES

The trainer needs to be alert with this exercise and constantly on the watch for participant safety.

Aliens

You are all extraterrestrial travellers (ETTs) and Earth robots (ERs) on a mission into deep space.

You have been captured and locked in cells by a group of renegade aliens from the planet Circo. Each group is locked in a separate cell (you are currently standing in your cell, the tape on the floor indicates the walls). Each group is made up of ETTs and one ER.

Be warned, at any time you may be taken out of your cell by the alien guards and executed.

Your only hope of escape is to order your ER to bring you the key to the cell. All the cells use the same key, which is in view. You will have to be quick about this though because some of the other cells hold enemy groups and if they escape first they may murder everyone else.

All of your ERs are made of a special material and are able to pass through the bars of your cell; therefore the ERs must be used to retrieve the key.

Before your ERs can be activated they need to be programmed. These are very early model ERs and they only have small memory banks. Their total capacity is 10 commands. Each command can be no more than 2 words. These sounds are the only sounds to which they will respond.

Another problem is that the aliens have had the foresight to remove the ERs' language chip; therefore, they cannot respond to any known language. They have also removed their voice chip so the ERs can no longer communicate verbally.

You will have to invent a language that the ERs can understand, for example, 'tutpoe' might mean 'turn right'. Once the new language has been formed it needs to be written on a piece of paper for the ERs to follow—this is their programming sheet.

Once the commands have been handed to the ERs they cannot be modified.

Good luck with your mission.

Planes Away

ITMXS

TIME REQUIRED	SIZE OF GROUP	MATERIAL REQUIRED
40–60 minutes.	Unlimited, but larger groups will have to be broken into smaller teams of 5 to 7 people.	One copy of the 'Planes Away—Instruction Sheet' and one copy of the 'Planes Away—Planning Sheet' for each team. Supplies of scissors, rulers, marking pens, and lots of A4 and A3 sheets of paper (use sheets ready to be recycled please).

Overview

An interesting and fun activity designed to demonstrate the value of planning.

Goals

1. To demonstrate to participants the value of planning.
2. To improve communication between participants.
3. To get participants moving.
4. To have fun!

Procedure

1. Split the large group into smaller groups of 5 to 7 people. Each group should have the same number of team members in it. Any participants left over can be additional observers for you to use.
2. Advise the teams that they will be participating in an exercise in which they will be required to produce paper planes to a set standard. The task will consist of 4 phases: phase 1—planning, phase 2—construction, phase 3—testing and selling, and phase 4—evaluation.
3. Give each team a copy of the 'Planes Away—Instruction Sheet' and the 'Planes Away—Planning Sheet'.
4. Tell the teams they now have 20 minutes (including reading the sheet) to complete phase 1: working out a costing, preparing a budget and completing the order form. At the end of phase 1 they are to hand their order forms to you to 'purchase' the necessary supplies.

5. After the 20-minute planning phase you should collect all completed order forms and distribute the materials requested. Once this is done, have the participants go into phase 2—the 5-minute construction phase (this needs to be a closely timed activity).
6. On completion of this phase, all planes are to be evaluated by the purchaser (phase 3). You will be the purchaser, along with any observers used.
7. After the final count has been carried out for each group, they should do their calculations to see what profit (or loss) they have generated (phase 4).
8. The team with the highest profit is declared the winner and a prize or certificate should be awarded.

Discussion points

1. Which group had the greatest profit (or perhaps the least loss)?
2. What assisted each group with this exercise?
3. What were some of the problems encountered?
4. How were these problems dealt with?
5. What roles did people take?
6. Would more planning time have been of use? Why? Why not?
7. How does this relate to the workplace?

Variations

1. In phase 2 all the participants could be blindfolded (obviously they would be told beforehand).
2. Times and/or costs may be modified.

TRAINER'S NOTES

Planes Away Instruction Sheet

The activity

Your team is to make paper planes to set standards using only materials purchased. At the end of the activity, your team will assess its performance according to the following criteria:
- the number of paper planes made to the specifications within a 5-minute period, and
- the number of paper planes actually made against the number planned.

The exercise is in 4 parts. The first phase is the planning phase. This will last for 20 minutes and will involve planning what you are going to do and what you will need to purchase (you will be able to borrow the hire equipment and 1 sheet each of A4 and A3 paper during the first phase, but they must all be returned before phase 2 commences). You will also need to elect a General Manager and decide on a team name during the first phase. The second phase will be the 5-minute construction phase. The next phase will involve testing and selling of the product. The fourth and final phase will be the evaluation phase.

The forms

Material costs are:

The fee to hire a pair of scissors for 5 minutes will be $20 (maximum 2 pairs per team)

The fee to hire a ruler for 5 minutes will be $15 (maximum 3 per team)

The fee to hire a marking pen for 5 minutes will be $10 (maximum 2 per team)

The cost to purchase 1 sheet of A4 paper is $1 per sheet

The cost to purchase 1 sheet of A3 paper is $1.80 per sheet

Teams purchasing more than 50 sheets of A4 or A3 paper will receive a 10% discount on the purchase price. Teams purchasing more than 100 sheets of A4 or A3 paper will receive a 20% discount on the purchase price.

Labour costs are $0.50 per minute for each person during production.

Contract

The following contract is offered for the purchase of the paper planes produced within the 5-minute construction period.

All planes must adhere to set standards. The standards are that:
- the planes must be produced using only A5 size pieces of paper (half A4 or one quarter A3)
- the planes are to have only cut edges, not torn edges
- all folds in the paper are to be neat and tidy
- each plane must have the team name written legibly on both wings
- each plane must be capable of flying more than 6 metres. This will be tested randomly by the purchaser after the construction phase.

Note: the purchaser will be responsible for evaluating the standards and their decision will be final and binding.

All paper planes constructed during phase 2, and meeting the above standards, will be purchased for $2 each.

Any shortfall in the number of planes produced and purchased, below the planned number, will incur a $2 fee per plane.

Planes Away Planning Sheet

Team name:

Planned costs

Equipment	Scissors	@$20/5 minutes
	Rulers	@$15/5 minutes
	Marking pens	@$10/5 minutes
Materials	A4 sheets of paper	@$1/sheet
		(less discount if applicable)
	A3 sheets of paper	@$1.80/sheet
		(less discount if applicable)
Labour	Minutes	@$0.50/person/minute

Planned sales

Total sales @ $2/plane

Planned profit/loss

Total sales
Total cost
Net profit/loss

- -

Order form

Team name:

Item	Quantity	Cost	Total
Scissors		@$20 each	
Rulers		@$15 each	
Marking pens		@$10 each	
A4 sheets of paper		@$1/sheet(1–50)	
A4 sheets of paper		@$0.90/sheet (51–100)	
A4 sheets of paper		@$.80/sheet (101+)	
A3 sheets of paper		@$1.80/sheet (1–50)	
A3 sheets of paper		@$1.62/sheet (51–100)	
A3 sheets of paper		@$1.44/sheet (101+)	

Total cost of materials

We aim to make _____ paper planes within the 5-minute construction phase and understand the fee for short deliveries.

Signed:_____ (for the team)

65

My Service Rules

IMPS

TIME REQUIRED	SIZE OF GROUP	MATERIAL REQUIRED
2–5 minutes.	Unlimited.	Each person will require a sheet of paper and a pen.

Overview

A relatively quick activity that can used on a course related to customer service.

Goals

1. To have the participants think about good customer service skills.
2. To recap on the key components of good customer service.
3. To energise the group.

Procedure

1. At the end of any customer service training have every participant grab a pen and paper.
2. Tell the participants to write their name vertically along the centre of their sheet of paper. This can be best demonstrated by writing your name on the whiteboard or flipchart.

3. Now ask the participants to write a good customer service action that fits in with each letter of their name. Again the best way to demonstrate this is on the whiteboard (see the next page for an example).
4. After everyone has completed their sheets, have each person read out what they have written.

Discussion point

What were the best rules suggested?

Variations

1. The finished sheets may be posted on the walls rather than read out.
2. A prepared overhead can be used effectively for step 3 (see the next page for an example).

TRAINER'S NOTES

My Service Rules

Give clear communication

Always acknowledge a request

always **R**espond to a request

learn to say **Y**es more often

66

Mid-course Questionnaire

CMXLPE

TIME REQUIRED	SIZE OF GROUP	MATERIAL REQUIRED
5–10 minutes.	Unlimited.	One copy of the 'Mid-course Questionnaire' and a pen for each participant.

Overview

This questionnaire can be used during training. It is best used midway through to allow you to refocus if necessary or modify your training plan.

Goal

To gain feedback from the participants midway through the training.

Procedure

1. At some predetermined point during the training, hand out a copy of the 'Mid-course Questionnaire' to each participant.
2. Ask the group to take a couple of minutes to answer the questions.
3. When all the sheets have been completed, collect them and review them during the next break.
4. After the break, highlight the main points raised and explain, if necessary, why some things are not possible.

Discussion points

None.

Variations

1. The questions can be shown on an overhead and participants asked to write comments on pieces of paper. These can be collected and reviewed.
2. The questions on the handout can be rewritten to suit the trainer.

TRAINER'S NOTES

Mid-course Questionnaire

Please take a minute to answer the questions below.

1. What do you really like about the course so far?

2. What do you really dislike?

3. Do you think anything has been overlooked (if so, what)?

4. Has anything been included that you feel is not relevant (if so, what and why do feel it is not relevant)?

5. If you had to present this course, would you do it any differently (if so, how)?

6. What questions would you like to ask?

7. Is there anything you would really like to change?

67

Most Valuable Things

TIME REQUIRED	SIZE OF GROUP	MATERIAL REQUIRED
5–10 minutes.	Unlimited.	One copy of the 'Most Valuable Things' handout and a pen for each person.

Overview

This activity may be used at the end of the course to gain feedback as to what the participants thought were the most valuable things they learned.

Goals

1. To gain feedback at the end of training on what the group considered the most valuable things learned.
2. To re-energise the group before leaving.

Procedure

1. Towards the end of training break the larger group into 2 smaller groups. One group should be identified as test team blue, and the other as test team orange.
2. Give each participant a copy of the 'Most Valuable Things' handout and a pen.
3. Ask the blue team to complete the top part of the handout. Tell the orange team that they are to complete the bottom part of the handout. The orange team is to list as many valuable things as possible before the blue team finishes (they can be told that the world record is 28 as an incentive).
4. When the blue team completes the puzzle, ask the orange team to read out what they have listed.
5. After the orange team finishes ask the blue team if they have anything to add to the list.

Discussion points

None.

Variations

1. A smaller group could be used in the blue team; this will allow more ideas to be generated by the orange team.
2. The orange team can be told that for each item they list there will be a one-minute credit on the finishing time.

TRAINER'S NOTES

Most Valuable Things

Blue team—please complete the following puzzle. You are to put a number in all 9 of the empty squares. You can only use the numbers 1, 3, 5, 7, 9, 11, 13, 15 and 17. Each number can only be used once. When completed, all the rows (vertical, horizontal and diagonal) must add up to the same total.

- -

Orange team—while the blue team complete their puzzle you are required to list all of the valuable things you have learned during this training. As soon as the blue team finishes you are to stop. We want you to beat the current record of 28 items so please use the back of the sheet as well.

_____

_____

_____

_____

_____

_____

_____

_____

_____

68

Daily Quiz

ITMXL

TIME REQUIRED	SIZE OF GROUP	MATERIAL REQUIRED
No time required during training.	Unlimited.	One copy of the 'Daily Quiz' for each person. A box to put all responses in. A prize for the winner.

Overview

This activity should be used on training courses that go for several days. It can also be used in the workplace on an ongoing basis.

Goals

1. To improve product knowledge.
2. To have fun.

Procedure

1. At the end of training each day hand out a copy of the 'Daily Quiz' to each participant.
2. Tell the group that they are to answer the questions and put their completed sheet into the box provided before the start of the next training session.
3. At the commencement of the next training session elect someone to draw a sheet from the box. The first correct sheet drawn is declared the winner and that person wins a prize.

Discussion points

None.

Variations

1. Can be done during coffee breaks rather than between training days.
2. Prearranged teams can be formed.

Solution

1. c)
2. b)
3. b)
4. a)
5. b)
6. b)
7. b)
8. c)
9. d)
10. b)
11. c)
12. d)
13. a)
14. d)
15. d)

TRAINER'S NOTES

You will design the first daily quiz, but subsequent ones will be designed by the participants. To do this, have participants form pairs at the commencement of the first training session. Randomly select the first pair. Tell them to design a quiz before the next training day. The quiz is to have 20 questions. Fifteen questions will be general knowledge and 5 questions must relate to the products and services their company provides. A new pair is selected each day, or a roster can be designed.

Daily Quiz (number 1)

1. How many bones make up the average skeleton?
   a) 186   c) 206
   b) 156   d) 286

2. What colour was the Skipper's shirt on 'Gilligan's Island'?
   a) Yellow   c) White
   b) Blue   d) Green

3. In the James Bond books, what is M's real name?
   a) Michael Minov
   b) Miles Messervy
   c) Malcolm Moore
   d) Monty Meysvery

4. In which country is the volcano Mount Unzen?
   a) Japan
   b) South America
   c) Norway
   d) Switzerland

5. How many fingers do the Simpsons characters have on each hand?
   a) 2   c) 4
   b) 3   d) 5

6. What was Fred Flintstone's bowling nickname?
   a) Twinkle steps
   b) Twinkle toes
   c) Twinkle feet
   d) Twinkle man

7. When was the 24-hour day introduced?
   a) 17th century BC
   b) 14th century BC
   c) 13th century BC
   d) 10th century BC

8. When was the watch invented?
   a) 1590   c) 1790
   b) 1690   d) 1890

9. How far is the sun from the earth?
   a) 126 400 000 kilometres/79 000 000 miles
   b) 141 300 000 kilometres/83 000 000 miles
   c) 142 400 000 kilometres/89 000 000 miles
   d) 148 800 000 kilometres/93 000 000 miles

10. What are the seven roman numerals?
    a) MHCLXVI
    b) MDCLXVI
    c) QMCLXZI
    d) QDCLXVI

11. What ship was Captain James Cook on when he reached Hawaii?
    a) Endeavour
    b) Restitution
    c) Resolution
    d) Bounty

12. Who was the last English king to be executed?
    a) Henry V
    b) George I
    c) Charles II
    d) Charles I

13. According to Monty Python, on what day does a lumberjack go shopping?
    a) Monday
    b) Tuesday
    c) Saturday
    d) Sunday

14. What is the largest planet in our solar system?
    a) Venus
    b) Pluto
    c) Saturn
    d) Jupiter

15. In what year was Robert Kennedy shot and killed?
    a) 1965
    b) 1966
    c) 1967
    d) 1968

69

Lottery Win

ITMXPS

TIME REQUIRED	**SIZE OF GROUP**	**MATERIAL REQUIRED**
15–30 minutes.	Unlimited, but a larger group will need to be broken into smaller groups of 3 or 4 people.	A copy of the 'How to Improve Our Performance' handout and a pen for each participant.

Overview

This is a fun, but serious, activity that can be used to help identify ways in which a company can be improved.

Goal

To identify ways of improving a company.

Procedure

1. Break the large group into smaller groups of 3 or 4 people.
2. Introduce this exercise by asking the group to imagine that last week they all shared a winning lottery ticket. Their total prize money was in excess of $5 000 000.
3. Last weekend the group got together and decided to invest all the money in the company they currently work for.
4. Advise each team that their task now is to make suggestions on what to do with the money so that they can get a greater return on their investment. They will have 10 minutes to complete their list of suggestions.

5. Give each participant a copy of the 'How to Improve Our Performance' handout.
6. After the 10 minutes each team should present their ideas. A vote may be taken and the group with the best ideas awarded a small prize or certificate.

Discussion points

1. Why is it that a lot of people don't think strategically within their own company?
2. Are any of the suggested improvements appropriate for our company to seriously consider? If so, what should we do with them?

Variations

1. This exercise can be done as an individual activity. Once the activity has been completed, have the participants form small groups and discuss the individual ideas.
2. The amount stated for the lottery win should be lower for smaller companies.

TRAINER'S NOTES

How to Improve Our Performance

1. _____
   _____

2. _____
   _____

3. _____
   _____

4. _____
   _____

5. _____
   _____

6. _____
   _____

7. _____
   _____

8. _____
   _____

9. _____
   _____

10. _____
    _____

70

Pre-course Interviews

ITFL

TIME REQUIRED	SIZE OF GROUP	MATERIAL REQUIRED
2 minutes per person at the beginning of the program.	Up to 15 people.	Each person needs to be given a copy of the 'This Is Your Life' handout well before the course begins.

Overview

This is a pre-course activity designed to make participants find out about each other before the course commences. It is good to use before a team-building program as it allows people to get to know each other outside of the workplace.

Goals

1. To allow the participants to find out about each other.
2. To develop a bonding approach to team building.
3. To give participants some pre-course work to carry out.

Procedure

1. Several days before the course commences distribute copies of the 'This Is Your Life' handout to all the participants.
2. Each participant is to interview a person nominated by you. The interviews are to be in-depth, but light-hearted. Humour should be encouraged.
3. Advise each participant that they will have to introduce their partner at the beginning of the training and reveal some of the highlights, or more interesting responses, from the interview. Each person will have 2 minutes to introduce their partner.

Discussion points

None.

Variation

For larger groups (up to 30 people) the introductions should be less than 1 minute each.

TRAINER'S NOTES

This interview technique helps participants get to know each other on another level. Often, team members know each other very well in the workplace, but have no idea what other people are like outside the office environment.

This Is Your Life

You will shortly be attending a training course. As a pre-course activity you are requested to interview one of the other participants. It is up to you to contact the person and conduct the interview.

Listed below are a few sample questions to get you going. Please feel free to modify these questions and add others. They are only given to get you started. During the beginning of training, you will be asked to give a 2-minute introduction on the other person highlighting all the interesting, and hopefully unusual, things you have discovered about them (present it with a 'This Is Your Life' theme). If you discover any humorous, or funny, stories about the person, please make sure you share them with the group during the introduction. Remember that you will only have 2 minutes to introduce them, not 30!

The person you will be interviewing is:

Sample questions to get you started.

1. What is your full name?
2. What was your background before starting with this company?
3. Where were you educated and what qualifications do you have?
4. Did you have a nickname at school? If so, what was it and how did you get it?
5. What is your partner's name, and what do they do?
6. Do you have any children? If so, how old are they and what are their names?
7. Do you have any pets? If so, how old are they and what are their names?
8. Do you have any hobbies or sports? If so, what are they?
9. What other interests do you have?
10. What would you consider to be something unusual about yourself?
11. What is your all-time favourite movie?
12. Who is your favourite actor?
13. What is your favourite song?
14. What is the best book you've ever read?
15. Which place would you most like to travel to for a holiday? Why?
16. Which place would you least like to travel to for a holiday? Why?
17. If you could live anywhere in the world, where would it be? Why?
18. What is your greatest success in life?
19. What are you most proud of?
20. If you could be anybody else (living or dead) who would you be, and why?
21. What is your greatest fear?
22. If you won a million dollars in the lottery next week, what would you do with it?
23. If you could invite any 3 people (living or dead) to a dinner party, who would they be, and why?
24. What frustrates you most in life?
25. What is the most embarrassing thing that has ever happened to you?
26.
27.
28.
29.
30.

71

Number Pyramid

IMX

TIME REQUIRED	SIZE OF GROUP	MATERIAL REQUIRED
2 minutes.	Unlimited.	One prepared 'Number Pyramid' overhead.

Overview

Another quick activity that can be used at any time during training.

Goals

1. To fill in time while people come back from breaks.
2. To develop a sense of competition.

Procedure

1. While waiting for the last few participants to return from a break, display the 'Number Pyramid' overhead.
2. Tell the group that they have to work out what the next line of numbers will be, and why.
3. The first person to give the correct answer should win a prize.

Discussion points

None.

Variations

1. This can be used effectively as a small group exercise.
2. A whiteboard could be used instead of the overhead.

Solution

13112221

Each new row of numbers is identified by reading out what is seen in the preceding row. What is read out is transcribed as the next row. For example, the first row is 1, this is read out as one one, and is written as '11', the next row is read out as two ones, and is written as '21' on the next line, this is read out as one two and one one and is written as '1211', etc.

TRAINER'S NOTES

Number Pyramid

1
11
21
1211
111221
312211
?

72

The Perfect Car

TCXP

TIME REQUIRED	SIZE OF GROUP	MATERIAL REQUIRED
20–30 minutes.	Up to 24 people. Larger groups will need to be broken into smaller groups of 5 to 7 people.	A copy of the 'Perfect Car' handout for everyone and a pen. Each team will also require a sheet of flipchart paper and a marking pen.

Overview

A quick brainstorming activity for small groups. This exercise is designed to address a number of issues such as problem solving, team building, teamwork and customer service skills.

Goals

1. To allow participants to identify some strategies in customer service.
2. To allow participants to practise some problem-solving techniques
3. To have the participants work as a team.
4. To have the participants share ideas.
5. To energise the group.

Procedure

1. Break the large group into smaller groups of 5 to 7 people.
2. Tell these groups that they represent companies that are going to produce a new motor vehicle. These companies will be competing for a lucrative contract to construct this motor vehicle for the next decade.
3. Advise each group that they have the task of listing all the features of this new vehicle. They will have 10 to 15 minutes to complete this list.
4. After each group has completed its list and given feedback on it, lead into a discussion on problem-solving strategies, teamwork, customer service skills, etc.

Discussion points

1. What was the problem? How was it broken down? Who did what?
2. Did any group approach other customers and ask them for their opinion? Why? Why not?
3. Do we always know what the customer wants?
4. How does this relate to our workplace?

Variation

You may decide to use a product more relevant to the group's needs.

TRAINER'S NOTES

The Perfect Car

What features are to be included in our 'perfect' vehicle?

Team Theme

IT

TIME REQUIRED	SIZE OF GROUP	MATERIAL REQUIRED
About 10–20 minutes depending on the number of teams.	The bigger the better, broken into smaller teams.	None.

Overview

This activity is for use on courses of longer duration, and with larger-sized groups. The large group should consist of established smaller groups or teams.

Goal

To develop a sense of team spirit.

Procedure

1. Before the training commences, the group needs to be broken into smaller teams. The teams should be workgroups that are already established. It doesn't matter if the teams are different sizes.
2. Tell each team that they are to present a team song at the beginning of the training. They will have from now until the first day of training to prepare.
3. The team with the best theme song should be awarded a prize.

Discussion points

None.

Variation

The briefing may be given at the beginning of the course and the teams advised that they will present their songs at some specific point during the training, perhaps at the start of the next day or at a dinner one evening.

TRAINER'S NOTES

Shoe Shop

TIME REQUIRED	SIZE OF GROUP	MATERIAL REQUIRED
2–5 minutes.	Unlimited.	None.

Overview

Here is another quick exercise that may be used while waiting for the last few participants to return from a break. It may also be used at the beginning of any training activities of a mathematical nature.

Goals

1. To keep participants occupied while waiting for stragglers to come back after a break.
2. To warm the group up when introducing training involving maths.

Procedure

1. During the beginning of training, or while waiting for the last few stragglers to come back from a break, read out the following story. On her way to work in the morning, Edna goes into a shoe shop and buys a pair of shoes that are on special for $12. Edna pays for the shoes with a $20 note. Eddie, the sales assistant, doesn't have any change at that time of the morning, so he runs next door to the sports shop and asks the owner, Enid, to change the $20 for smaller notes. Eddie returns to the shoe shop and gives Edna her $8 change. Later in the day Enid comes in to see Eddie and is very upset. She has found that the $20 is a counterfeit and has informed the police. Eddie feels bad about this, so he apologises to Enid for all the trouble that has been caused and

takes $20 out of the cash register and gives it to Enid. They both now sit and wait for the police to arrive.

2. Ask the group how much cash Enid and Eddie have each lost (not including the stock value of the shoes). The participants are to write their answers down and not show them to anyone.
3. After several minutes, ask each participant what they have written. This will show how people perceived the information differently.

Discussion points

1. Why did some people have different answers?
2. If used as a small group exercise (see Variation section), ask how many people would have been able to answer the question by themselves?
3. How does this relate to the training we are about to start?

Variation

The story can be read (once) for all participants to listen to, then the briefing can be given. Rather than have each individual write their answer, form sub-groups of 3 or 4 people and get the group to give an answer. This will also demonstrate the benefit of synergy.

Solution

Enid lost nothing and Eddie lost $8.

TRAINER'S NOTES

This exercise works well after Game 62, which could be used before the previous break. It should demonstrate that some people are now using a different approach to their problem-solving techniques.

Minefield

TCMXS

TIME REQUIRED	SIZE OF GROUP	MATERIAL REQUIRED
15–30 minutes.	12 or more (the more the better).	A blindfold for each pair. A prepared minefield. Indoors, this can be done by placing 1 long strip of masking tape at each end of the room and positioning open sheets of newspaper on the floor. The tape indicates the start and finish of the minefield, while the sheets of newspaper are the mines (lots of sheets should be used, the more the better). Outdoors, 2 lengths of rope can be used, and sheets of newspaper.

Overview

This team activity can be used indoors or outdoors. It allows team members to build trust and improve communication.

Goals

1. To build trust within the team.
2. To improve communication among participants.
3. To energise the group.

Procedure

1. Ask everyone to form pairs.
2. Tell each pair to go to one end of the room and line up.
3. Give one person in each pair a blindfold and ask them to put it on.
4. Once the blindfolds are in place, and the participants are out of the main open area, place the masking tape on the floor and lay out the sheets of newspaper.
5. When this is done, explain to the group that there is a minefield in front of them.
6. Tell the pairs that the people without blindfolds have been captured and are not allowed to move. They also know the exact location of all the mines in the minefield. The people with blindfolds have

been able to escape, but it's the middle of the night and pitch black outside so they cannot see anything at all.

7. Advise each pair that the person without the blindfold has to give their partner verbal directions for crossing the minefield. Should the blindfolded escapee touch any of the mines, it's all over.
8. Explain that sunrise isn't too far away and, as a result, the exercise will need to be completed quickly. When it becomes light, the guards will be able to see anyone left in the minefield and they will be shot.
9. Tell the group that it's time to go and that you wish them luck.

Discussion points

1. Who was first to cross?
2. How did everyone feel about this exercise?
3. How clear were the directions?
4. What problems were there?
5. How does this apply in the workplace?

Variation

The minefield can be covered with mouse traps, lego blocks or anything else that might represent a mine.

TRAINER'S NOTES

You need to be very observant with this exercise, both for safety reasons and to see if anyone touches the sheets of newspaper. Should any person not want to participate, use them as extra observers. With a larger group this exercise can become quite loud. That's an advantage as it becomes confusing as to where directions are coming from and who they are directed at.

Spring-clean

ITFMXLPS

TIME REQUIRED	SIZE OF GROUP	MATERIAL REQUIRED
20–30 minutes.	Unlimited, but large groups will need to be broken into smaller groups of 5 to 7 participants.	Each team will require a sheet of flipchart paper and pens.

Overview

It seems that everyone has done an 'Inbasket' exercise these days, so here is something a bit different. It's a team-building/time-management activity that can be used at any time during training.

Goals

1. To develop a team approach to problem solving.
2. To improve time-management techniques.

Procedure

1. Break the large group into smaller groups of 5 to 7 people.
2. Advise the groups that they are going to be given a task to complete.
3. Tell them that Spring is just around the corner, and it's time to get ready for the annual spring-clean.
4. Each team must formulate a list of activities that would be performed when preparing to spring-

clean a home. Each activity on the list needs to be prioritised. The list (in priority order) is to be compiled in 10 minutes.
5. After the task has been completed have one person (from each team) give a presentation on their final list.

Discussion points

1. How did the team arrive at a consensus in the time frame allocated?
2. How were the priorities set? What criteria were used?
3. How were any differences resolved?
4. How does this exercise apply at home or in the workplace?

Variation

Other activities can be used rather than spring-cleaning.

TRAINER'S NOTES

77

Slash Equals What?

IMX

TIME REQUIRED	SIZE OF GROUP	MATERIAL REQUIRED
2 minutes.	Unlimited.	One prepared 'Slash Equals What?' overhead.

Overview

Another quick activity that can be used at any time during training.

Goals

1. To fill in time while people come back from breaks.
2. To develop a sense of competition.

Procedure

1. Display the 'Slash Equals What?' overhead while waiting for the last few participants to return from a break.
2. Advise the group that they have to tell you which of the 6 words shown is the missing one and why. Also let the group know that the first person to give you the correct answer wins a prize.

Discussion points

None.

Variations

1. This can used effectively as a small group exercise.
2. A whiteboard could be used rather than the overhead.

Solution

/ = Why

When one straight line is added to each of the letters on the left-hand side of the equation it converts the figure to the word sound.

I = Eye
B = Be
Q = Queue
R = Are
T = Tea, and so
Y = Why

TRAINER'S NOTES

Slash Equals What?

T = EYE
3 = BE
0 = QUEUE
P = ARE
1 = TEA
/ = ?

? = SOAP, FOUR, WHY, TO, RUN OR SOUP

78

Number Logic

TMX

TIME REQUIRED	SIZE OF GROUP	MATERIAL REQUIRED
25 minutes to introduce plus time to solve (this can vary dramatically between groups).	Unlimited.	Each team will require a copy of the 'Number Logic' handout and a pen.

Overview

Here is an exercise to get everyone in the group thinking. It can be used for teamwork, energising or simply for fun.

Goal

1. To demonstrate the benefit of using a team to solve a problem.
2. To have some fun.
3. To give participants a problem to solve overnight on courses of longer duration.

Procedure

1. Introduce this activity by telling the group that they are going to be given a problem to solve.
2. Ask the participants to form teams of 3 or 4 people.
3. Give each group a copy of the 'Number Logic' handout.
4. Tell the teams that they have to arrange each of the numbers and signs in the top row into each blank row and column to arrive at the answers shown. Point out that all calculations must be made stage by stage.
5. The first team to give the correct answer should be awarded a small prize.

Discussion points

1. What helped the team solve this problem?
2. What hindered the team in solving this problem?
3. Why can teams solve this type of problem more easily than individuals?
4. How does this affect us in the workplace?

Variations

1. Can be done individually, but may take a lot of time to process.
2. Can be given as a problem-solving activity for teams to work on overnight on longer courses.

Solution

4	×	9	+	2	-	3	=	35
×		-		+		×		
2	+	3	×	9	-	4	=	41
+		×		×		+		
3	-	2	×	4	+	9	=	13
-		+		-		-		
9	+	4	×	3	-	2	=	37
=		=		=		=		
2		16		41		19		

TRAINER'S NOTES

142

Number Logic

4	×	9	+	2	-	3	=	35
	■		■		■		■	■
							=	41
	■		■		■		■	■
							=	13
	■		■		■		■	■
							=	37
=	■	=	■	=	■	=	■	■
2	■	16	■	41	■	19	■	■

79

What Can I Sell You?

ICMXS

TIME REQUIRED	SIZE OF GROUP	MATERIAL REQUIRED
5–10 minutes.	Unlimited.	A prepared 'What Can I Sell You?' overhead transparency.

Overview

Here is an activity that may be used on a sales course to encourage participants to think about features and benefits.

Goal

To have participants focus on a product's features and benefits.

Procedure

1. When anyone during the training talks about the features of a product you can mention that customers tend to buy products based on benefits rather than features. In other words, what the product can do for them or what it allows them to do.

2. Give at least one example such as, 'Our time-management training course has been rated as the best in the world. That's a feature. The benefit is that it will allow you to finish work on time and enjoy more time with your family and friends'.

3. Ask the group for other examples.

4. Next, show the participants the 'What Can I Sell You?' overhead.

5. Ask them to form pairs and work out the features and benefits of each item.

6. Have each pair quickly state to the group what they decided the features and benefits were for each item.

Discussion points

1. What are the features and benefits of our products or services?

2. Are the benefits obvious to our potential customers?

Variation

Once the initial activity has been completed, a prepared overhead of all the participants' products and services can be shown, and the pairs asked to list the features and benefits of each item.

TRAINER'S NOTES

What Can I Sell You?

A computer

A coffee cup

A car

A pet dog

A plant

A lottery ticket

A pen

An apple

A television

A book

A training course

Reincarnation

ITM

TIME REQUIRED	SIZE OF GROUP	MATERIAL REQUIRED
Less than 1 minute per person.	Up to 30 people.	None.

Overview

This icebreaker helps people get to know each other a little better.

Goal

To get the participants to know each other better.

Procedure

During a standard introduction ask everyone the following question: 'If it were possible for you to be anyone else, living or dead, who would you be, and why?'.

Discussion points

1. Did that give a better insight into other people?
2. Is there any participant you would like to talk to further (during the breaks) about their suggested reincarnation?

Variation

For groups larger than 30, have participants form small groups and discuss, within the group, who they would want to be.

TRAINER'S NOTES

A Bag of Laughs

ITMS

TIME REQUIRED	SIZE OF GROUP	MATERIAL REQUIRED
10 minutes.	Unlimited, but a large group will need to be broken into smaller groups of 3 or 4 people.	None.

Overview

This activity can be used at the start of training as a self-disclosure exercise.

Goals

To have participants disclose information about themselves to a small group.

Procedure

1. Break the large group into smaller groups of 3 or 4 people.
2. Explain to the group that everyone carries a bag, briefcase, wallet, or purse, and that their contents often reveal a lot of information about the owner.
3. Ask the participants to get their own bags, briefcases, wallets, or purses and reveal the contents to the rest of their group. Some items may need explaining as they are revealed.
4. You should participate in this activity.

Discussion points

1. Did you find out anything interesting about the other participants in your group?
2. Who had the most unusual item?

Variation

There is no need to break the group up if there is a smaller number of participants.

TRAINER'S NOTES

Vacation Time

ITFMXLPS

TIME REQUIRED	SIZE OF GROUP	MATERIAL REQUIRED
20–30 minutes.	Unlimited, but large groups will need to be broken into smaller groups of 5 to 7 participants.	Each team will require a sheet of flipchart paper and pens.

Overview

It seems that everyone has done an 'Inbasket' exercise these days, so here is something a bit different. It's another team-building/time-management activity that may be used any time during training.

Goals

1. To develop a team approach to problem solving.
2. To improve time-management techniques.

Procedure

1. Advise the group that they are going to be given a task to complete.
2. Ask them to form groups of 5 to 7 people.
3. Tell them that last year, when they went on holidays, things were a bit chaotic before they left. Some of them were totally disorganised and everyone had had enough before the holiday had even begun!
4. As a result, each team must come up with a list of activities that will help the participants pre-pare for their next annual holiday. Each activity on the checklist is to be prioritised. The list (in priority order) is to be completed in 10 minutes.
5. At the end of the 10 minutes, ask one person (from each team) to give a presentation on their final list.

Discussion points

1. How did the team arrive at a consensus in the time frame allocated?
2. How were the priorities set? What criteria were used?
3. How were any differences resolved?
4. How does this exercise apply at home or in the workplace?

Variation

Other activities can be used other than a checklist for holidays.

TRAINER'S NOTES

Quick Review

MLE

TIME REQUIRED	SIZE OF GROUP	MATERIAL REQUIRED
2 minutes.	Unlimited.	None.

Overview

This activity may be used as a quick review before each break to ensure learning is taking place.

Goal

To conduct a quick review of the items covered since the last break.

Procedure

1. Just before each break, ask the group to tell you 5 things they have learned or discovered since the previous break. Let them know that if they can't come up with 5 items, the coffee break will be cancelled!
2. As each item is called out, acknowledge it, and count down until you have the required total.

Discussion points

None.

Variations

1. Number of items is at your discretion.
2. Items called out may be listed on a whiteboard.

TRAINER'S NOTES

Line Up

ITM

TIME REQUIRED	SIZE OF GROUP	MATERIAL REQUIRED
2 minutes.	Unlimited.	None.

Overview

Here is another way of breaking a large group down into smaller groups.

Goals

1. To break a large group into smaller groups with a random mix.
2. To get participants moving.

Procedure

1. Inform the participants that they are going to break into smaller groups for the next activity.
2. Ask them to form a straight line with the person with the smallest shoe size at one end of the line, and the person with the largest at the other. Everyone is to put themselves in the correct order.
3. Advise the group that this is to be carried out as a nonverbal exercise.
4. When the line has been formed you can divide it into the number of groups required.

Discussion point

Did everyone find the correct position?

Variations

1. May be conducted without the nonverbal rule.
2. May be conducted with eyes closed or blindfolds on.

TRAINER'S NOTES

85

Magic Coins

ITMX

TIME REQUIRED	SIZE OF GROUP	MATERIAL REQUIRED
5 minutes.	Unlimited, but a large group will need to be broken into smaller groups of 3 or 4 people.	One prepared sheet of paper with a hole in it for each group and a coin. The hole should be in the centre of the sheet and be about 25% smaller than the coin itself.

Overview

Here is a quick problem-solving exercise for small groups.

Goals

1. To demonstrate the benefit of synergy.
2. To fill in time while waiting for the last few people to come back from a break.

Procedure

1. Break the large group into smaller groups of 3 or 4 people.
2. Give each group their sheet of paper and their coin.
3. Explain to the groups that their task is to get the coin through the hole without tearing the paper.
4. The first team to complete the exercise can be awarded a small prize.

Discussion points

1. Why is it easier for some teams to solve problems?
2. What made it easier to solve this?
3. What made it harder?
4. How can this apply in the workplace?

Variation

Can be done individually.

Solution

Fold the sheet of paper in half with the fold going through the centre of the hole. Hold the paper up in a 'V' shape with the V pointing down. Place the coin inside the paper so that it's sitting in the hole. Gently pull at the bottom outside edges of the V so that it starts to open. The coin will fall through the hole without tearing it.

TRAINER'S NOTES

Nicknames

TIME REQUIRED	SIZE OF GROUP	MATERIAL REQUIRED
No extra time required.	Unlimited.	None.

Overview

This activity can be used at the very start of training while the participants are introducing themselves.

Goal

To have participants disclose something about themselves.

Procedure

When the participants are introducing themselves at the beginning of training, ask them to tell the group what nickname they used to have at school (or at home) when they were a child, and how they got it.

Discussion points

None.

Variation

May be used as an exercise before a coffee break.

TRAINER'S NOTES

A Free Lunch

TCXLPS

TIME REQUIRED	SIZE OF GROUP	MATERIAL REQUIRED
A lunchbreak, plus debriefing time.	6 to 12 people.	Money to pay for lunch for everyone. Each person may be given a copy of the 'Free Lunch' handout before going on their break. Each group will require flipchart paper and a pen after lunch.

Overview

Here is an activity that includes a free lunch. It's a good exercise that deals with customer service issues.

Goals

1. To observe and give feedback on good and bad customer service skills.
2. To have a free lunch!

Procedure

1. At the end of the morning session let everyone know that lunch is your treat today.
2. Tell the group that this will be kind of a working lunch though. Everyone will be able to enjoy themselves, but they will need to be observant.
3. Let the group know that during lunch they are to observe anything that relates to either good or bad customer service. Advise the group not to discuss their observations during the lunchbreak, but to wait until they get back to the training room.
4. If the 'Free Lunch' handout is used, suggest to the participants that they take a pen and make a few notes as they see things.

5. When back in the training room, ask the group to list all the good things they saw and the areas that could be improved on.
6. A discussion could then be led into the areas of self-improvement and improvement for their organisation.

Discussion points

1. What did you see that you felt was good?
2. What did you see that you felt was exceptional?
3. Did you see anything that you felt needed improvement?
4. What was the best thing you saw?
5. What was the worst thing you saw?
6. How does this relate to both you and your organisation?

Variations

1. The group may be sent on a shopping errand rather than going to lunch.
2. If a large group is involved it would be better to break them into smaller teams and send them to different locations. Each sub-group could then give feedback to the larger group.

TRAINER'S NOTES

Free Lunch

Good techniques observed	Opportunities for improvement

88

Trivia Review

XLE

TIME REQUIRED	SIZE OF GROUP	MATERIAL REQUIRED
5 minutes.	Unlimited.	A prepared handout with legitimate questions and trivia questions on it. The trivia questions are to be mixed in with the legitimate questions. If you have 10 legitimate questions (scoring 10 points each), and 10 trivia questions (scoring 10 points each), it makes it possible for a person to have a potential score of 200% (although we would like 100% as a minimum). Games 8 and 68 will give you some ideas for trivia questions to ask. A small prize should also be used.

Overview

This activity can be used as a course-evaluation questionnaire with a difference.

Goal

To gain feedback from the participants.

Procedure

1. Before the end of training, create the test questionnaire. The questionnaire should have 10 legitimate questions (to test what people have learned during training) mixed in with 10 trivia questions.

2. At the conclusion of training hand a copy of the questionnaire to each person along with a pen.
3. Tell the group that they must now complete the final test for the course, and that the person with the highest score will be given a prize.

Discussion points

None.

Variation

Can also be used as a mid-course quiz.

TRAINER'S NOTES

89
Staff Turnover

TMXP

TIME REQUIRED	SIZE OF GROUP	MATERIAL REQUIRED
15–20 minutes.	Unlimited, but large groups will need to be broken into smaller groups of 5 to 7 people.	None.

Overview

This is an exercise to get the group thinking of ways to increase productivity and reduce staff turnover. It can be used in supervision or management training.

Goal

To generate ideas on reducing staff turnover.

Procedure

1. Break the large group into smaller groups of 5 to 7 people.
2. Inform the groups that the CEO of their company has requested that they generate ideas to help reduce staff turnover.
3. There are no budget constraints, but the ideas have to be realistic and practical. The participants have 10 minutes to produce as many ideas as possible.

4. After all the groups have finished, ask each group to give a presentation on the ideas they have generated.
5. The group creating the best ideas (or perhaps the most ideas) should be awarded a prize.

Discussion points

1. What were the best ideas?
2. Are these ideas realistic?
3. Why aren't they being done now?
4. Should you pursue them further?

Variation

Can be started as an individual exercise. Small teams could then be formed for group discussion and the generation of other ideas.

TRAINER'S NOTES

90

Team Profile

TIME REQUIRED	**SIZE OF GROUP**	**MATERIAL REQUIRED**
45–60 minutes.	Unlimited, but large groups will need to be broken into smaller groups of 5 to 7 people.	Each person will require a copy of the 'Team Profile' handout and a pen.

Overview

This exercise is designed to make a team look at itself and see where its performance can be improved.

Goals

1. To have a team analyse itself.
2. To improve a team's performance.
3. To discuss areas of weakness in a team.

Procedure

1. Give out copies of the 'Team Profile' handout to all the participants.
2. Now ask the group to think about their team and how it performs.
3. Each participant should then complete the 'Team Profile' handout based on their own observations.
4. After all the forms have been completed, break the larger group into small groups of 5 to 7 people and have each person discuss their individual responses.
5. Advise the groups that they are to suggest improvements for any item that has been marked in the 2 right-hand columns.
6. Each sub-group should report back to the larger group with its suggestions.

Discussion points

1. Which areas are we happy with?
2. Which areas stood out the most as needing improvement?
3. How can we improve these areas?
4. What steps can we carry out tomorrow to get these improvements started?

Variations

1. Step 4 can be done as one large group, but it will take longer to process.
2. The 'Team Profile' handout can be given out as pre-course work for the participants to do before starting the training.

TRAINER'S NOTES

Team Profile

Please rate your team on the following items	Excellent	Very good	Good	Fair	Poor
1. Clarity of team goals.					
2. Commitment to work towards set goals.					
3. Clarity of individual roles.					
4. Effectiveness of team meetings.					
5. Relationship between team members.					
6. Relationship with external clients/suppliers.					
7. Leadership skills of team leader.					
8. Ability to work together as a team.					
9. Attitude of team.					
10. Recognition for team performance.					
11. Recognition for individual performances.					
12. Problem-solving skills.					
13. Suitability of resources used to do the job.					
14. Communication between team members.					
15. Feedback on team performance.					
16. Quality of team's output.					
17. Ability to innovate.					
18. Knowledge and skills of team members.					
19. Willingness to take appropriate risks.					
20. Ability to have fun.					

Additional comments:

Academy Awards

ME

TIME REQUIRED	SIZE OF GROUP	MATERIAL REQUIRED
5 minutes.	Unlimited.	A certificate for each area identified.

Overview

An activity that can be used as part of the final closure for the training.

Goal

To have a fun closure.

Procedure

1. At the beginning of training let the group know that there will be an awards presentation at the end of the course.
2. Tell the group that, at the end of training, they will be asked to nominate, and vote for, people who have excelled in various areas such as:
   – Best role-play
   – Best question asked
   – Best tip given
   – Best overall performance
   – Best demonstration
3. At the end of training ask for nominations for each category.
4. When nominations have closed, a vote should be taken to see who the winners are.
5. Award each winner with a certificate.

Discussion points

None.

Variation

Form an Academy Awards Committee at the start of training and let them control the whole process.

TRAINER'S NOTES

Certificate

CONGRATULATIONS

(person's name) _____

you have been awarded the

(name of award) _____

AWARD

Signed: _____

Problem-solving Cycle

TXLS

TIME REQUIRED	SIZE OF GROUP	MATERIAL REQUIRED
2–5 minutes.	Unlimited.	One prepared 'Problem-solving Cycle' over-head.

Overview

An exercise to establish the rules for problem solving.

Goal

To give participants a set of rules to follow when looking for solutions to problems.

Procedure

1. Ask the group if they would like to see a formula for solving problems.
2. Show the group the 'Problem-solving Cycle' over-head and explain each of the steps.

Discussion points

1. How do you currently solve problems?
2. Will this cycle work in all situations?
3. Can all problems be solved?

Variation

A handout can be used instead of the overhead.

TRAINER'S NOTES

Problem-solving Cycle

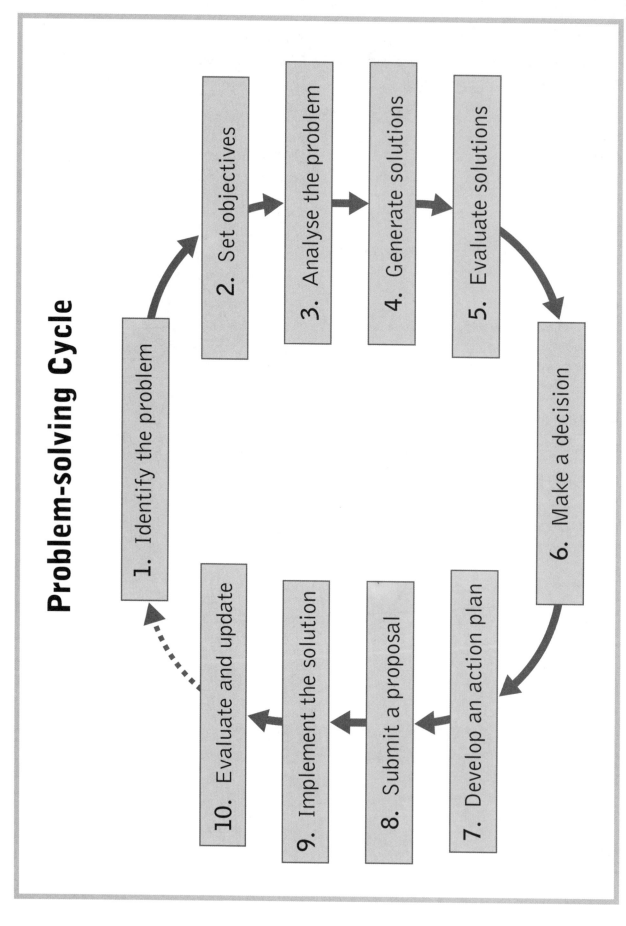

1. Identify the problem
2. Set objectives
3. Analyse the problem
4. Generate solutions
5. Evaluate solutions
6. Make a decision
7. Develop an action plan
8. Submit a proposal
9. Implement the solution
10. Evaluate and update

Popping Prizes

IM

TIME REQUIRED	SIZE OF GROUP	MATERIAL REQUIRED
No extra time required.	Unlimited.	Balloons with folded slips of paper inside them. The slip of paper will have a prize written on it. The balloons should be inflated and attached to a wall in the room.

Overview

If you have a problem choosing who gets what prize, this game will help solve the dilemma.

Goal

To help determine who gets what prize.

Procedure

1. As games are conducted and winners identified, give the winner a pin and ask them to select a balloon (participants are only allowed to select a balloon if they get a pin from you).

2. When the winner has made their selection they are to pop it and see what the prize is.

Discussion points

None.

Variation

Pins can be given to participants who make outstanding contributions as the training progresses.

TRAINER'S NOTES

Guess Who I Saw?

I

TIME REQUIRED	SIZE OF GROUP	MATERIAL REQUIRED
2–5 minutes, depending on the size of the group.	Unlimited.	None.

Overview

A quick icebreaker that can be used early on in the training.

Goals

1. To help the participants get to know each other.
2. To encourage communication.

Procedure

1. During the beginning of training, usually after the introductions, tell the group about someone famous you bumped into (who it was and how it happened).
2. Now ask the group if anyone else has bumped into someone famous. If they have, find out who it was and how it happened.

Discussion points

None.

Variation

With a small group, you could go round asking the participants about the most famous person they have ever seen in real life.

TRAINER'S NOTES

95

Sacred Cows

TCXPS

TIME REQUIRED	SIZE OF GROUP	MATERIAL REQUIRED
30–45 minutes.	Unlimited, but larger groups will need to be broken into smaller groups of 3 to 6 people.	None required, but a picture of a cow would be appropriate (but not necessary).

Overview

This activity is great for identifying outdated policies, procedures and practices.

Goal

To have participants identify outdated policies, procedures or practices, and look at suggestions for improvement.

Procedure

1. At an appropriate point during training get the group to break into sub-groups of 3 to 6 people.
2. Ask each group to think of outdated policies, procedures or practices in their own area (these are referred to as sacred cows). Some examples may include wasting money, purchasing the wrong equipment, upsetting customers, taking too long to process orders, or simply abiding by the old maxim, 'we've always done it this way, why should we have to change?'. Tell the groups to list their sacred cows in priority order, and then list ways of improving or modifying them.

3. At the end of 15 minutes ask each group to present a summary of their identified sacred cows and the suggestions they have made to improve the situation.
4. All ideas and suggestions should be collated by you and passed on to the appropriate people.

Discussion points

1. Is it possible to change any of these things?
2. How can we go about making these changes?
3. Who do we need to pass the ideas on to?
4. Why was the procedure done that way initially?

Variation

This is a great activity that can be used on an ongoing basis. You may want to suggest to the group that this activity become part of their normal team meeting.

Source

Adapted from Kriegel, Robert, Brandt, David, **Sacred Cows Make the Best Burgers**, Harper, Sydney, 1996.

TRAINER'S NOTES

96

Up-selling

CXS

TIME REQUIRED	**SIZE OF GROUP**	**MATERIAL REQUIRED**
10–15 minutes.	Unlimited, but large groups will need to be broken into pairs.	A copy of the 'Up-selling' handout for each pair.

Overview

This sales exercise is designed to get participants thinking about up-selling products to their clients.

Goal

To have participants think of ways to up-sell their products and services.

Procedure

1. During sales training ask the participants to form pairs.
2. Advise the pairs that they are going to be involved in an up-selling exercise (up-selling means that the customer purchases more than they originally asked for). For example, a customer may want to purchase 3 boxes of widgets but may be given the option of purchasing 5 boxes and getting an additional 10% discount or the chance to win a weekend away.
3. The group should be asked for other examples.

4. Once the group understands what up-selling is all about, distribute copies of the 'Up-selling' handout and ask the pairs to practise up-selling techniques on each other.
5. Wander around and select the best skills displayed.
6. After everyone has had enough practice, ask the best players to demonstrate to the group.
7. If it is appropriate, ask the participants what products or services they could up-sell in the workplace, and how they could go about doing it.

Discussion points

1. What have people tried to up-sell you recently?
2. Is there anything wrong with up-selling? Is the customer better or worse off?
3. What products and services can you up-sell in your organisation?

Variation

Can be done in small groups of 3 or 4.

TRAINER'S NOTES

Up-selling

Scenario A

The stationery company you work for has a special this month on pens. If a customer purchases 12 or more boxes of pens, they get a free mouse pad. A customer has just phoned you to order 6 boxes of pens. See if they might be interested in the special.

Scenario B

A customer has just come in to the shop to purchase a hamburger and fries. Your boss has a special on at present where a customer can get a hamburger, fries and a drink for just 20 cents more. See if they might want the combo instead.

Scenario C

You work in a computer store. A customer has come in and is asking for prices on different packages. There are two packages that they seem interested in, one is $200 dearer but has extra software in the price (the extra software has a value of $500 and you think that it may be of use to the customer based on their requirements). See if they might be interested in the more expensive package.

Scenario D

You work in a motor repair shop. A customer has just come in and wants a tune-up on their car. Your company has a deal where they can have a tune-up, wheel rotation and tyre balance for an extra $10. See if they might be interested.

Scenario E

You work in a company that builds and sells houses. A young couple have come in and are very keen to purchase but you know that price is very important to them. They are looking at a basic 3-bedroom model. For an extra $4000 they can have the next model up which is the same but includes a lock-up garage and an extra bedroom. See if they might be interested.

Scenario F

A customer has just come in to your nursery to purchase 20 plants at $5 each. A bulk rate of $3 each applies for purchases of 50 plants or more. See if they might be interested.

97

Letterman List

LE

TIME REQUIRED	SIZE OF GROUP	MATERIAL REQUIRED
5–10 minutes.	Unlimited, but will need to be broken into smaller groups of 4 to 8 people.	A pen and paper for each person.

Overview

This activity may be used at the end of training to gain feedback from the participants as to what they considered the most valuable things learned on the course.

Goals

1. To gain feedback from the group at the end of training on what they thought were the most valuable things learned.
2. To re-energise the group before leaving.

Procedure

1. Towards the end of training, break the larger group into smaller groups of 4 to 8 people. The group size isn't important and will depend solely on the total number of participants.

2. All participants should be given a sheet of paper and a pen.
3. Ask the groups to identify the 10 most important things they learned from the training.
4. Advise everyone that they will have to list the items and do a David Letterman style presentation (i.e. number 10 is ...) and work their way up to number 1. Drum rolls can be included if necessary.

Discussion points

None.

Variations

1. Smaller or larger groups can be used.
2. Each group could be given a piece of flipchart paper and a marking pen. They can then reveal their top 10 as they go along.

TRAINER'S NOTES

98

Bag Scavenger Hunt

ITMS

TIME REQUIRED	SIZE OF GROUP	MATERIAL REQUIRED
5–10 minutes.	Unlimited, but a large group will have to be broken into smaller groups of 6 to 10 participants.	A copy of the 'Scavenger Hunt' handout for each team.

Overview

This is a fun activity that helps people get to know each other better.

Goals

1. To have participants share information about themselves to a small group.
2. To liven the group up.
3. To see how resourceful some team members are.

Procedure

1. Break the large group into teams of 6 to 10 people.
2. Tell the participants that they are going to be involved in a scavenger hunt, and that a prize will be awarded to the winning team. All the items must currently be in their possession, that is, in bags, pockets, briefcases, wallets, or purses. If the teams don't have an item on them, they cannot go and find it. Each item on the list is worth 1 point.
3. Hand out copies of the 'Scavenger Hunt' sheet to each team and give them 2 minutes to collect as many items as they can.

Discussion points

1. Which group had the highest score?
2. Which group had the lowest score?
3. Which group had the greatest number of 'unusual' items?

Variation

Can be done as a mid-course energiser.

TRAINER'S NOTES

Scavenger Hunt

You are required to collect the following items from possessions you currently have with you. The time limit and point system will be explained during the briefing.

- [ ] A black comb
- [ ] A $100 note
- [ ] A 2-cent coin
- [ ] A used postcard
- [ ] A gold credit card
- [ ] An Avis Preferred Renter card
- [ ] A Hertz #1 club card
- [ ] A restaurant receipt from another state
- [ ] A Seiko watch
- [ ] A lace handkerchief
- [ ] A brochure from a hardware store
- [ ] A family photo
- [ ] A 9-volt battery
- [ ] An umbrella
- [ ] A scuba certification card
- [ ] A plane ticket
- [ ] A chocolate
- [ ] An unused postage stamp
- [ ] A condom
- [ ] A bank statement
- [ ] A business card without writing on the back of it
- [ ] A parking ticket
- [ ] A blank cheque
- [ ] A ball
- [ ] An analogue phone
- [ ] A roll of sticky tape
- [ ] A bookmark
- [ ] A solar calculator
- [ ] A computer disk
- [ ] A CD
- [ ] A receipt for an item of clothing
- [ ] A matching pen and pencil set
- [ ] A book with more than 500 pages
- [ ] A laser pointer
- [ ] A sock
- [ ] A box of matches
- [ ] A Swiss army knife
- [ ] A pair of sunglasses
- [ ] A Christmas card

99

Line Up II

ITM

TIME REQUIRED	SIZE OF GROUP	MATERIAL REQUIRED
2 minutes.	Unlimited.	None.

Overview

Here is another way of breaking a large group down into smaller teams.

Goals

1. To break a large group into smaller groups with a random mix.
2. To get participants moving.

Procedure

1. Inform the group that they are going to break up into smaller groups for the next activity.
2. Explain to the group that you need them to form a straight line with the person with the least amount of time at the company at one end, and the person with the most at the other.

3. Everyone now puts themselves in the correct order.
4. The whole process is to be carried out as a nonverbal exercise.
5. When the line has been formed, divide it into the number of groups required.

Discussion point

Did everyone find the correct position?

Variations

1. May be conducted without the nonverbal rule.
2. May be conducted with eyes closed or blindfolds on.

TRAINER'S NOTES

100

Responses

TIME REQUIRED	SIZE OF GROUP	MATERIAL REQUIRED
2–5 minutes depending on how much information is required.	Unlimited.	One handout (either the 'Training Evaluation Sheet', the simple 'Course Evaluation Sheet' or the more complex 'Course Evaluation Sheet') for each person.

Overview

It seems that trainers can never have enough response forms or evaluation sheets ('happy sheets' as they are called in the industry). Here are three more to add to the collection.

Goals

1. To gain feedback from participants on the training content.
2. To gain feedback from participants on your performance.
3. To gain feedback from participants on other relevant (and sometimes not so relevant) parts of the training.

Procedure

1. Select the response form that best suits your requirements.
2. Hand the sheet out to participants at the end of training.
3. Once the forms have been filled in collect them. The results can be summarised and the information passed on to the relevant people.

Discussion points

None.

Variations

You may modify the forms to suit your own needs.

TRAINER'S NOTES

Training Evaluation Sheet

I value your feedback. Please respond candidly to the following questions and rate the workshop on each criterion listed below.

Course title: _____

Your name: _____ (optional)

	Exceeded expectations	Met expectations	Needs improvement	Not applicable
Training content				
Organisation of material	☐	☐	☐	☐
Presentation level	☐	☐	☐	☐
Relevance to my job	☐	☐	☐	☐
Quality of handouts	☐	☐	☐	☐
Small group activities	☐	☐	☐	☐
Visual aids	☐	☐	☐	☐
Presentation				
Presentation style	☐	☐	☐	☐
Trainer's knowledge	☐	☐	☐	☐
Coverage of material	☐	☐	☐	☐
Responses to questions	☐	☐	☐	☐

Suggestions for improvements: _____

_____

Other comments: _____

_____

Please tick the rating that best reflects your overall evaluation of this course.

Excellent ☐   Very good ☐   Good ☐   Fair ☐   Poor ☐

Course Evaluation Sheet

Your name: _____ (optional)

Course/program: _____

1. Did the course meet your needs or reasons for attending?

☐ Yes　　　　　　　　Comments: _____

☐ No　　　　　　　　_____

☐ Didn't have any　　_____

2. How would you rate the information presented:

☐ Too advanced/difficult　Comments: _____

☐ Just right　　　　　　_____

☐ Too simple/elementary　_____

3. How relevant was the course to your job or other needs?

☐ Very relevant　　　Comments: _____

☐ Relevant　　　　　_____

☐ Not relevant　　　_____

4. What did you like most about the course? _____

_____

_____

5. What did you like least about the course? _____

_____

_____

6. Would you like to suggest any modifications to the program? _____

_____

_____

7. Please rate the proficiency of the course leader/s in their duties.

☐ Excellent　　　　Comments: _____

☐ Good　　　　　　_____

☐ Fair　　　　　　_____

☐ Poor

8. Overall, how would you rate this course?

☐ Excellent　　　　Comments: _____

☐ Good　　　　　　_____

☐ Fair　　　　　　_____

☐ Poor

9. We would appreciate any other comments or reactions you have towards the program or the course leader/s. Please use the space below.

_____

_____

_____

_____

_____

Thank you for taking part in the program and for taking the time to give us your feedback.

Course Evaluation Sheet

Your name: _____ (optional)

Course/program: _____

	5 Excellent	4	3 Satisfactory	2	1 Poor
Course effectiveness					
1. Overall quality of course content (i.e. concepts, tools, information, ideas presented)	☐	☐	☐	☐	☐
2. Overall quality of materials (i.e. handouts, media used, etc.)	☐	☐	☐	☐	☐
3. Course objectives met	☐	☐	☐	☐	☐

For any item above marked 3 or less, please provide additional information.

	5	4	3	2	1
Trainer effectiveness					
1. Presentation skills (i.e. organisation, use of examples, use of visual aids, etc.)	☐	☐	☐	☐	☐
2. Management of the learning environment (i.e. time, group interaction, etc.)	☐	☐	☐	☐	☐
3. Interaction with participants (i.e. responding to question, etc.)	☐	☐	☐	☐	☐
4. Overall effectiveness of trainer	☐	☐	☐	☐	☐

For any item above marked 3 or less, please provide additional information.

	5	4	3	2	1
Administration					
1. Course location, time, etc.	☐	☐	☐	☐	☐
2. Registration process	☐	☐	☐	☐	☐
3. Learning environment (i.e. facilities, furnishings, lighting, temperature, etc.)	☐	☐	☐	☐	☐

For any item above marked 3 or less, please provide additional information.

	5	4	3	2	1
Overall learning experience					
1. Overall relevance to job	☐	☐	☐	☐	☐
2. Overall reaction to this learning experience	☐	☐	☐	☐	☐
3. I would recommend this course to others	YES ☐		NO ☐		

For any item above marked 3 or less, please provide additional information.

Additional comments:

101

Briefcase Clean Out

TIME REQUIRED	SIZE OF GROUP	MATERIAL REQUIRED
10–15 minutes.	Unlimited.	Each participant will require a pen and paper. A large garbage bin may come in handy.

Overview

This exercise can be used for sales training or time-management training.

Goal

To have the participants clean out their briefcase or whatever bag they carry.

Procedure

1. Start this exercise by asking the participants to list everything they currently have in their brief-case or bag.
2. After this has been done you should explain that people often carry around too many surplus items.
3. Advise the group that they will be going on an overseas sales call and will only be allowed to take 5 items with them from their list.
4. Ask the participants to select their 5 items and then pick a partner to discuss their choices with.
5. Once everyone has completed their discussions, they are to get their briefcase or bag and clean it out (this is what the big bin is for).

Discussion points

1. Why is it that we carry so much stuff with us?
2. How can we avoid this in future?

Variations

1. The second part of step 4 can be done as a group discussion.
2. Step 5 can be skipped if necessary.

TRAINER'S NOTES

102

1 + 1

ITMX

TIME REQUIRED	SIZE OF GROUP	MATERIAL REQUIRED
5 minutes.	Unlimited, but a large group will need to be broken into smaller groups of 3 or 4 people.	One prepared 'Maths Test' overhead.

Overview

Here is another quick problem-solving exercise for small groups.

Goals

1. To demonstrate the benefit of synergy.
2. To fill in time while waiting for the last few people to come back from a break.

Procedure

1. Break the participants into groups of 3 or 4 people.
2. Tell the teams that they are going to be involved in a quick problem-solving activity.
3. Now advise the teams that the overhead they are about to see has 20 calculations on it. Fifteen of the calculations are correct and 5 are incorrect.

4. The team with the first correct answer will be declared the winner and awarded a prize. Calculators are not to be used.

Discussion points

1. What made it easier for teams to solve this problem?
2. What made it harder?
3. What plan of attack was used?
4. How can this apply in the workplace?

Variations

1. Can be done individually.
2. One calculator per group may be allowed.

Solution

2, 4, 8, 15, and 20 are incorrect

TRAINER'S NOTES

Maths Test

1. $\sqrt{225} = 15$	2. $13 \times 15 = 185$	3. $32 \times 7 - 42 = 182$	4. $56 \times 56 - 86 = 3005$	5. $pi = 3.1416$
6. $1265 \div 5 = 253$	7. $(27 - 6) + (9 \div 3) = 24$	8. $((82 \times 43) \div 2) = 1736$	9. $26 + 93 - 42 = 77$	10. $12 \times 60 \times 60 = 43\,200$
11. $18\,216 \div 72 = 253$	12. $24 \times 7 \times 365 = 61\,320$	13. $42 \times 7 = 294$	14. $\sqrt{144} = 12$	15. $45 \times 4 + 50 = 320$
16. $\sqrt{3136} = 56$	17. $\sqrt{729} + 6 = 33$	18. $2997 \div 3 = 999$	19. $1 + 8 + 100 + 1 = 110$	20. $((256 \div 2) - 8) = 126$

103

No-word Crossword

CFPS

TIME REQUIRED	SIZE OF GROUP	MATERIAL REQUIRED
15–20 minutes.	Unlimited, as long as everyone can see the demonstration.	Two copies of the 'No-word Crossword' and a pen. One blindfold will also be required.

Overview

This exercise will show participants that their verbal instructions may not always be as clear as they think.

Goals

1. To demonstrate to participants that their verbal instructions may not always be as clear as they think.
2. To allow participants to see that a task needs to be broken down into small segments for instructional purposes.
3. To allow participants to see that even simple instructions must involve two-way communication.

Procedure

1. Start this exercise by asking for 2 volunteers.
2. When the volunteers have been selected, ask one of them to leave the room and wait outside until further notice.
3. Give the remaining volunteer a copy of the 'No-word Crossword'.
4. Tell them that when the other person is brought back into the room they are to give them a set of verbal instructions to complete the maze. To successfully do this the blindfolded person will have to get their pen and go from the 'Start' to the 'Finish' while making the minimum number of errors (an error occurs when they put their pen line into a black area).

5. Place the other copy of the 'No-word Crossword' on a table along with a pen. Place a chair in front of the table.
6. Now go outside and retrieve the other volunteer. Before bringing them back in, ask them to put the blindfold on. Sit them down and let both volunteers know that this will be a one-way communication process in that the person giving the instructions can speak, but the person doing the task must remain totally silent.
7. The person should then start giving instructions.

Discussion points

1. How many mistakes were made?
2. How did the blindfolded person feel during this exercise?
3. How did the person giving the instructions feel during the exercise?
4. Can instructions be given effectively using one-way communication?
5. If an instruction is not carried out correctly, who is at fault?
6. What can we do to make our instructions clearer and easier to understand?

Variations

1. After debriefing the activity, it is often worthwhile repeating the exercise to see the range of improvements.
2. This exercise can be done in pairs.

TRAINER'S NOTES

Ensure that the person outside isn't given too much information at the start. All the instructions should be given by their partner when they come back into the room. When bringing the blindfolded person back into the room, be aware of any safety issues.

No-word Crossword

START

FINISH

Sample Observer's Sheets

The attached 'Observer's Sheets' are to be used as sample designs. They have been included as reference for you to design your own 'Observer's Sheets'. It is important when you use observers that they know exactly what it is they are supposed to be observing.

By using a properly designed observation sheet you are ensuring consistency. You are also ensuring that all the points you want raised will be covered in the final discussion phase.

Observer's Sheet No. 1

It is your task to record what happens in chronological order. Record the time in the left-hand column, your observation in the centre column and who was involved in the third column.

Do not take part in the exercise, pass any comment or make any suggestions. The information you provide after the exercise will assist the whole group to discover things that are directly relevant to the way in which they operate.

Time	Observation	Name

Observer's Sheet No. 2

It is your task to record appropriate points under the headings listed below.

Do not take part in the exercise, pass any comment or make any suggestions. The information you provide after the exercise will assist the whole group to discover things that are directly relevant to the way in which they operate.

Was the exercise planned?

How was it planned?

Were people organised?

...ources used?

...ed?

...d?

...e take?

...e communication?

...recording?

Observer's Sheet No. 3

It is your task to record appropriate points under the headings listed below.

Do not take part in the exercise, pass any comment or make any suggestions. The information you provide after the exercise will assist the whole group to discover things that are directly relevant to the way in which they operate.

How was the exercise analysed?

Were people organised?

Were objectives set?

Were tasks properly delegated?

Were all available resources used?

How was the group led?

Were problems solved?

How effective was the communication?

How were alternatives discussed and evaluated?

What else was worth recording?

Observer's Sheet No. 1

It is your task to record what happens in chronological order. Record the time in the left-hand column, your observation in the centre column and who was involved in the third column.

Do not take part in the exercise, pass any comment or make any suggestions. The information you provide after the exercise will assist the whole group to discover things that are directly relevant to the way in which they operate.

Time	Observation	Name

Observer's Sheet No. 2

It is your task to record appropriate points under the headings listed below.

Do not take part in the exercise, pass any comment or make any suggestions. The information you provide after the exercise will assist the whole group to discover things that are directly relevant to the way in which they operate.

Was the exercise planned?

How was it planned?

Were people organised?

Were objectives set?

Were all available resources used?

Was the time controlled?

How was the group led?

What roles did people take?

How effective was the communication?

What else was worth recording?

Observer's Sheet No. 3

It is your task to record appropriate points under the headings listed below.

Do not take part in the exercise, pass any comment or make any suggestions. The information you provide after the exercise will assist the whole group to discover things that are directly relevant to the way in which they operate.

How was the exercise analysed?

Were people organised?

Were objectives set?

Were tasks properly delegated?

Were all available resources used?

How was the group led?

Were problems solved?

How effective was the communication?

How were alternatives discussed and evaluated?

What else was worth recording?

Further Reading

Below is a list of publications that can be used as sources for more training games. This list also includes publications that contain some theoretical background behind training and the use of games.

All of the publications are valuable, but some are more relevant than others. The symbols shown to the left of the titles have been included to give the reader a guide as to the relevance of these books to our topic of training games. The key to the symbols is shown below.

Reference key

✪ Read this one and put it in your library; it's a great training games resource.

★ Read this one if you need more information or ideas on training games or other associated areas.

☆ Read this one if you've got nothing else to do.

While some of these titles are fairly old, remember that a game designed in sixth-century India (chess) can still be very useful, and a lot of fun. Training games never die, they just get modified.

★ ADAIR, John, **Effective Teambuilding**, Pan Books, London, 1987.

☆ BAKER, Pat, MARSHALL, Mary-Ruth, **More Simulation Games**, The Joint Board of Christian Education of Australia and New Zealand, Melbourne, 1977.

☆ ———, **Using Simulation Games**, 2nd Edition, The Joint Board of Christian Education of Australia and New Zealand, Melbourne, 1982.

★ BENDALY, Leslie, **Strength in Numbers**, McGraw-Hill Book Company, Toronto, 1997.

✪ BISHOP, Sue, **Training Games for Assertiveness and Conflict Resolution**, McGraw-Hill, Inc., New York, 1977.

☆ BRAMLEY, Peter, **Evaluating Training Effectiveness**, McGraw-Hill Book Company, London, 1997.

✪ BURNARD, Philip, **Training Games for Interpersonal Skills**, McGraw-Hill, Inc., New York, 1992.

✪ CARLAW, Peggy, DEMING, Vasudha, **The Big Book of Customer Service Training Games**, McGraw-Hill, Inc., New York, 1999.

★ CARRIER, Michael, **Take 5: Games and Activities for the Language Learner**, Harrap Limited, London, 1983.

☆ CHARNEY, Cy, CONWAY, Kathy, **The Trainer's Tool Kit**, Amacon, New York, 1997.

✪ CHRISTOPHER, Elizabeth M., SMITH, Larry E., **Leadership Training Through Gaming**, Nichols Publishing Co., New York, and Kogan Page Limited, London, 1987.

☆ CLARK, Neil, **Team Building**, McGraw-Hill Book Company, London, 1994.

★ CONNER, Gary, WOODS, John, **Sales Games and Activities for Trainers**, McGraw-Hill, Inc., New York, 1997.

☆ **ELT Documents: Games, Simulations and Role-Playing**, The British Council English Teaching Information Centre, London, 1977.

★ FLUEGELMAN, Andrew (ed.), **More New Games**, Doubleday, New York, 1981.

✪ FORBESS-GREENE, Sue, **The Encyclopedia of Icebreakers**, University Associates, California, 1983.

✪ GREENWICH, Carolyn, **The Fun Factor**, McGraw-Hill, Inc., New York, 1997.

☆ HARRINGTON-MACKIN, Deborah, **The Team Building Tool Kit**, Amacon, New York, 1994.

✪ HARSHMAN, Carl, PHILLIPS, Steve, **Team Training**, McGraw-Hill, Inc., New York, 1996.

★ HONEY, Peter, **The Trainer's Questionnaire Kit**, McGraw-Hill, Inc., New York, 1997.

✪ KIRK, James, KIRK, Lynne, **Training Games for the Learning Organisation**, McGraw-Hill, Inc., New York, 1997.

✪ KROEHNERT, Gary, **100 Training Games**, McGraw-Hill Book Company Australia, Sydney, 1991.

✪ ——, **101 More Training Games**, McGraw-Hill Book Company Australia, Sydney, 1991.

✪ ——, **102 Extra Training Games**, McGraw-Hill Book Company Australia, Sydney, 2000.

★ ——, **Basic Presentation Skills**, McGraw-Hill Book Company Australia, Sydney, 1998.

✪ ——, **Basic Training for Trainers**, 2nd Edition, McGraw-Hill Book Company Australia, Sydney, 1994.

★ ——, **Taming Time: How Do You Eat an Elephant?**, McGraw-Hill Book Company Australia, Sydney, 1998.

★ MILL, Cyril R., **Activities for Trainers: 50 Useful Designs**, University Associates, California, 1980.

★ MYERS, Scott, BARBATO, Carole, **The Team Trainer**, Irwin, Chicago, 1996.

✪ NEWSTROM, John W., SCANNELL, Edward E., **Games Trainers Play**, McGraw-Hill, Inc., New York, 1980.

✪ ——, **The Big Book of Team-Building Games**, McGraw-Hill, Inc., New York, 1998.

☆ ODENWALD, Sylvia, **Global Solutions for Teams**, Irwin, Chicago, 1996.

✪ PFEIFFER, J. William, JONES, John E., **A Handbook of Structured Experiences for Human Relations Training**, Volumes 1–10, University Associates, California, 1975–85.

★ ROHNKE, Karl, **Cowstails and Cobras II**, Kendall/Hunt Publishing Company, Iowa, 1989.

★ ——, **Silver Bullets**, Kendall/Hunt Publishing Company, Iowa, 1984.

✪ SCANNELL, Edward E., NEWSTROM, John W., **More Games Trainers Play**, McGraw-Hill, Inc., New York, 1983.

★ ——, **The Big Book of Presentation Games**, McGraw-Hill, Inc., New York, 1998.

★ SILBERMAN, Mel (ed.), **The 1997 McGraw-Hill Team and Organisational Development Sourcebook**, McGraw-Hill, Inc., New York, 1997.

★ ——, **The 1997 McGraw-Hill Training and Performance Sourcebook**, McGraw-Hill, Inc., 1997.

★ TUBESING, Nancy Loving, TUBESING, Donald A., **Structured Experiences in Stress Management**, Volumes 1 and 2, Whole Person Press, Duluth MN, 1983.

★ ——, **Structured Exercises in Wellness Promotion**, Volumes 1 and 2, Whole Person Press, Duluth MN, 1983.

✪ TURNER, David, **60 Role-plays for Management and Supervisory Training**, McGraw-Hill, Inc., New York, 1992.

☆ VAN MENTS, Morry, **The Effective Use of Role-play**, Kogan Page Limited, London, 1983.

✪ VILLIERS, Peter, **18 Training Workshops for Leadership Development**, McGraw-Hill, Inc., New York, 1993.

★ WILSON, George, **Team Member's Survival Guide**, McGraw-Hill Book Company, New York, 1997.

✪ WOODCOCK, Mike, **50 Activities for Teambuilding**, Gower Publishing Company, England, 1989.

☆ WRIGHT, Andrew, BETTERIDGE, David, BUCKBY, Michael, **Games for Language Learning**, Cambridge University Press, Cambridge, 1979.

TRAINING INFORMATION

We offer a comprehensive range of training services around the world. If you would like more information on our training services, please complete the information below and forward it to us by mail, fax or email.

Name: _____

Position: _____

Company: _____

Address: _____

_____

_____

Phone: _____

Fax: _____

Email: _____

I would like more information on:

☐ In-house Presentation Techniques Skills Seminar

☐ Public seminar information for Presentation Techniques Skills Workshops

☐ In-house Training Techniques Workshops

☐ Public seminar information for Training Techniques Workshops

☐ In-house Time Management Seminars

☐ Public seminar information for Time Management Seminars

☐ Public seminar information on other subjects

☐ In-house Training Games Workshops

Post to: Gary Kroehnert
                Training Excellence
                PO Box 3169
                Grose Vale, NSW 2753
                Australia

Or fax to: (02) 4572 2200

Or email: doctorgary@hotmail.com

ORDER FORM

McGraw-Hill

Phone: (02) 9415 9888   Fax: (02) 9417 7003
http://www.mcgraw-hill.com.au/mhptr
OR MAIL THIS ORDER FORM

	0.07.470434.6	Greenwich	The Fun Factor	37.95
	0.07.470770.1	Greenwich	Fun & Gains	32.95
	0.07.470606.3	**Kroehnert**	**Basic Presentation Skills**	**32.95**
	0.07.470662.4	**Kroehnert**	**Taming Time**	**32.95**
	0.07.452770.3	**Kroehnert**	**100 Training Games**	**37.95**
	0.07.470749.3	**Kroehnert**	**101 More Training Games**	**37.95**
	0.07.470802.3	**Kroehnert**	**102 Extra Training Games**	**37.95**
	0.07.470913.5	**Kroehnert**	**Basic Training for Trainers 3/e**	**37.95**
	0.07.470768.X	Leigh & Kinder	Learning Through Fun & Games	37.95
	0.07.471051.6	Leigh & Kinder	Fun & Games for Workplace Learning	37.95
	0.07.470842.2	Zeus & Skiffington	The Complete Guide to Coaching at Work	32.95

NAME

TITLE

COMPANY

ADDRESS

POSTCODE

Payment Details

I enclose payment by (please tick):

☐ Cheque   ☐ Credit Card   ☐ Company Purchase Order

☐ Bankcard   ☐ American Express ☐ Mastercard   ☐ Visa   ☐ Diner's Club

Card Number ☐☐☐☐☐☐☐☐☐☐☐☐☐☐☐☐   Expiry Date ☐☐☐☐

SIGNATURE

Phone, fax or mail your order to

McGraw-Hill Australia Pty Ltd

4 Barcoo Street Roseville NSW 2069 Ph: (02) 9415 9888 Fax: (02) 9417 7003

Email: cservice_sydney@mcgraw-hill.com.

Please ensure you have enclosed payment with your order. If you fax your order, please do not post it as well.